UMBRIA

Peter McClure 1994

Forests

Principal ... of wine pro...

△ Thermal s...

Nórcia
Cáscia
Sordo
Corno
Corno
Nera
Foligno
Sellano
Trevi
Teverone
Montefalco
Bevagna
Spoleto
Acquasparta
Massa
Martana
Todi
Terni
Narni
Amélia
Lago di Piediluco
Lago di Corbara
Lago di Alviano
Nestore
Tevere
Chiani
Parrano
Città di Pieve
Castel Viscardo
Orvieto
Lago di Bolsena
Tévere (Tiber)
Nera

L A Z I O

Kilometres

0   10   20

In the Valley of the Fireflies

PETER HOBDAY

In the Valley of the Fireflies

An Englishman In Umbria

ILLUSTRATED BY KATE DICKER

MICHAEL JOSEPH
LONDON

MICHAEL JOSEPH LTD

Published by the Penguin Group
Penguin Books Ltd, 27 Wrights Lane, London w8 5tz
Viking Penguin Inc., 375 Hudson Street, New York, New York 10014, USA
Penguin Books Australia Ltd, Ringwood, Victoria, Australia
Penguin Books Canada Ltd, 10 Alcorn Avenue, Toronto, Ontario, Canada m4v 3b2
Penguin Books (NZ) Ltd, 182–190 Wairau Road, Auckland 10, New Zealand

Penguin Books Ltd, Registered Offices: Harmondsworth, Middlesex, England

First published in 1995
Copyright © Peter Hobday Productions 1995

Set in 10.5/14pt Monophoto Plantin Light
Filmset by Datix International Limited, Bungay, Suffolk
Printed in England by Clays Ltd, St Ives plc

A CIP catalogue record for this book is available from the British Library

ISBN 0 7181 0080 8

The moral right of the author has been asserted

'This was among my prayers: a piece of land not so very large, where a garden should be and a spring of ever-flowing water near the house and a bit of woodland as well as these.'

Horace, *Odes*

'Journeys, like artists, are born and not made. A thousand differing circumstances contribute to them, few of them willed or determined by will – whatever we may think. They flower spontaneously out of the demands of our natures – and the best of them lead not only outwards in space, but inwards as well. Travel can be one of the most rewarding forms of introspection.'

Lawrence Durrell, *Bitter Lemons*

Contents

1 Umbria Beckons

THE FIRST INKLING of a journey came before sun-up, months before I even set eyes on a place called Umbria, a place I must confess I had never even heard of. But let me start at the very beginning and give you some background. The early morning call from the BBC comes at four a.m. The phone usually only needs two rings before I manage to locate the receiver by the side of the bed. At first I used to leave the phone outside the bedroom to force me out of bed and, more important, force me awake. Now, after nearly fourteen years in the job of presenting the *Today* programme, the discipline is such that once awake I stay awake. Even so, despite all these years before the radio mast, it is still a shock, and my system resents the intrusion on what is normally the deepest sleep period of the night.

Whichever *Today* programme production assistant it is who has to make the wake-up calls, Janet, Marcia, Lorraine or

Vanessa, they are no nonsense and to the point.

'It's four o'clock, Peter.'

'Is anything happening?' I usually ask.

'Not much,' they say.

Even if the third world war had started, they would still say 'not much'. One morning Lorraine told me seven fire bombs had gone off in central London, 'but that's all, no one was hurt'. I suppose for many people, being pulled from sleep at such a time with such information, it might have prompted more conversation. But we like to think we are professionals. What's more the team will have been working all night, booking lines around the world, arranging cars to pick up contributors, typing scripts, getting Britain's favourite morning programme into shape. The overnight editor and the other two producers, one of whom will be in the studio making sure than everything runs to the second, will have been endlessly discussing who we should talk to about this or that development. They will also be cursing the 'day team' for not setting up this or that story properly. Of course, they do it partly tongue in cheek because, as the weeks run on, they will move from nights to days and will become the day team that someone else castigates for its shortcomings.

The *Today* programme is a 24-hour-a-day operation, working pretty well seven days a week. It has the biggest morning audience bar none, including television. It sets the political agenda day in and day out, and the interviews with cabinet ministers and leading political figures usually dominate the headlines for the rest of the day. What's more, they are usually 'live', that is, done there and then in real time so the audience can hear the triumphs and the mistakes either of interviewer or interviewee. All of which puts the whole team under special pressure. Working on the *Today* programme there is no hiding place from the six or seven million people who tune in every morning. Your postbag, either collectively or individually, makes sure you are never complacent, that there is always another side to the story but, most of all, chiding you for mutilating the language and being lazy in your choice of words.

'You really ought to know the difference between a contagious disease and an infectious disease,' wrote one irate customer on the back of a postcard with a 'words fail me' cartoon on the front.

The presenters have the task of fronting the whole team's efforts in the studio, coping with any changes to the running order, handling breaking stories and sudden changes of direction. One memorable morning, the then prime minister, Mrs, now Lady, Thatcher, rang just before seven to correct the impression given by Mikhail Gorbachev's spokesman that he was going straight back home to the Armenian earthquake, missing out on a scheduled trip to London. The prime minister felt that suggested that the call on her in London was of no consequence and could be dropped at a minute's notice. The night team thought it was a hoax call and put the phone down after thanking the caller. When the phone rang again, the night editor said, 'I knew it was number ten that time, it was the way the telephone rang the second time that convinced me.'

All of which makes the job, whatever your role on the programme, exciting and testing. You may just about be on the point of talking to the young woman who thinks she has seen the Loch Ness Monster, when they say in your ear via the talk-back system between the control desk and the studio, 'We've got the home secretary,' and within seconds you are discussing his reaction to the latest figures that show, despite the rising prison population, crime itself is rising even faster. The team do their best to brief but in the end you are on your own, using the knowledge you've acquired over the years of reporting from around Britain and around the world, of the stories you've covered, and the fact that you read most newspapers most days, watch TV news bulletins and listen to radio news wherever you are. We are all news junkies, hooked on the state of the world and the politicians' response to it.

All this is not without cost in your private life. If you are lucky, the family will put up with early nights and early mornings, with the television or radio switched on to news whenever it happens and listened to or watched in silence.

Family and friends will put up with your ego, which persists outside the studio, no matter how much you try to control it. It's a heady business making a small name for yourself and having a huge audience every day when you go to work. But it's wearing . . . the disturbed sleep pattern, the need to keep up with the news and, above all, the need to be able to perform in top gear as soon as the programme begins. After a few weeks you have a form of jet lag, as if you have been commuting to New York and back every week. You start to sleep at odd hours. And you can get tetchy if people are long-winded in explanation. The three-minute interview is all you need and so you tend to interrupt people who take more than thirty seconds explaining anything. Casual conversations become interviews. If you are not careful you withdraw into the world of broadcasters and journalists, and rarely see 'real people'.

Despite such drawbacks, I wouldn't really do any other job and, in broadcasting, there are really no other daily broadcasting jobs to do after *Today*. But like the politicians we interview, the job can never be permanent. I've had a good run for nearly fourteen years but it will end sometime. I watched Brian Redhead work flat out until the end . . . almost dreading the day when he couldn't, in his phrase, 'drop a word in the ear of the nation'. Tragically, Brian died before he could enjoy another life, maybe even another career. We had often talked, he and

I, about leaving the programme. There was but a handful of years between us in age. What do you do after *Today*? How will we spend all our tomorrows? What next?

Once past my fiftieth birthday the question nagged away in my mind, especially on those nights before the programme when, as sometimes happens, you just cannot get to sleep and the more you worry, the more you stay awake.

The question was brought home to me most forcefully about the time Mrs Thatcher was trying not to let on she'd had ten years in office. She knew that sooner or later . . . and it was sooner . . . people would say, 'She's been around too long, it's time for a change . . .' I was coming up to ten years and I thought I'd better start making my plans now . . .

It was in this frame of mind that the idea of actively preparing for a new life after *Today* took root. But, instead of just giving up the one for the other, I wanted to try and run the two lives in parallel: one that was active and pressured, the other that was calm and provided space. A vague plan – but it made me receptive to the idea of getting a place abroad; in short, how I came eventually to buy nearly two acres of brown earth in Umbria in central Italy.

Part of the idea for such a transition came from an article on how the Japanese salaryman is given one day off a week five years before retirement; then a second day off a week the next year, until finally he is only working one day a week in his last year. I did not want to suffer the fate of so many men . . . and soon professional women too no doubt, of turning up my toes within months of stopping work because of boredom. I remember a headline in a business magazine over an article on retirement: 'The Day the Telephone Stops Ringing.' One minute it's all go, the next full stop. Now flexitime and the rest will allow us to construct a double life as we change from full-time work to full-time retirement.

Except you don't retire. What my partner and I did has surprised us, enthralled us and, more often than we care to admit, stretched us almost to breaking point. And there's still so much more to do. Now, as I survey my little plot in Umbria, with the shade trees, the fruit, the herbs, the vegetables, and taste the first oil from my olives on a tomato salad made from my own tomatoes and fresh basil from the pot under the vine, I know it was worth every moment. As Lawrence Durrell wrote: 'Journeys . . . are born not made. A thousand differing circumstances contribute to them, few willed or determined by will – whatever we may think. They flower spontaneously out of the demands of our natures – and the best of them lead us not only outwards in space but inwards as well. Travel can be one of the most rewarding forms of introspection.'

Durrell says these thoughts came to him at dawn in Venice, on a ship which was to carry him down through the islands to Cyprus. My journey did not start in such a magical way, at some precise moment when the mind is able to ponder the mysteries of human existence, nor was it a moment that I can pinpoint with such accuracy. My journey started more prosaically in the *Today* office at about four-thirty one March morning. As always, I was working my way through the morning papers, seeing what idiocies the world had got up to while I had been asleep. I had got half-way through the *Daily Telegraph*, when an item on the property page caught my eye. I don't have the cutting, I haven't bothered to get the exact date, but it was early 1987. The item said that there were properties available in Umbria and Tuscany which could still be had for a song. These deserted farmhouses were now being put on the market in increasing numbers. Tuscany was still relatively expensive, it being a more fashionable destination, but the discerning buyer should look further south to Umbria or across the mountains to the Marche, that wild part of Italy on the eastern side of the Apennines.

As Durrell says, 'a thousand differing circumstances contribute to journeys': in my case, my idle thoughts about life after *Today* and the fact that my widowed mother had died peacefully in her 84th year leaving her only surviving son a small cottage in Burnham on Sea and a little cash. Burnham is one of those relics of a Victorian era, when the middle classes started to take an annual holiday. After my father died, my mother moved there from Wolverhampton where I was brought up. She was born in Bristol and wanted to move back to the west country. She found this little two-up, two-down terraced cottage near the sea front. It had no garden, her only disappointment, but allowed her to make a new life, new friends, and I'm sure it extended her life by several years.

Comfortable though the Burnham house was, it was too small for me and the family, and Burnham itself was not the most marvellous of places as far as I was concerned. My late brother John, also a broadcaster in his day, once described it on the BBC's World Service as a place 'where even the restaurants close for lunch'. I had travelled too much in my professional life to want to settle in a little Somerset backwater. My late wife, Tamara, a Parisian, had always planned for us to go back to France in retirement. But her death from cancer at the early age of forty-seven made the idea of France without her impossible. But still the yearning to go somewhere other than Britain was there and my new partner, Victoria, daughter of an army officer, had followed the colours when she was young – to Africa and India and the Middle East and so had wanderlust too. Victoria was as keen as I that we find somewhere in the sun. You see how the 'circumstances' build.

So here's this piece in the *Telegraph*, months after my mother's death, with an idea tailor-made for the Hobdays as a way to use the small inheritance, start a new phase in our life somewhere else and build our future a step at a time, literally and metaphorically, brick by brick. I called home and woke Victoria up. I have to pay tribute to her self-control, as I excitedly told her what I had seen and asked her to call the agent mentioned in the article, a Yorkshireman called Steve Emmet.

The programme came and went, the usual round of interviews, a ritual insult with the sports man Gary Richardson, a quick cup of coffee and a slice of toast with Sue MacGregor afterwards, and off we went our separate ways. By the time I got home, I had forgotten about my pre-dawn call to Victoria. But here's another of Durrell's circumstances. Because the man came from Yorkshire and so does Victoria, she felt she could trust him and had called. He was sending her a list of possible properties within our price range, and would be in London in a couple of days' time.

From then on events moved pretty fast. With her usual determination Victoria got the details, talked to other agents, wrote to other agencies, and within weeks said, 'If you are serious about this project, then the best thing to do is to take a trip to Italy which these local agents will arrange for us.' If this were a novel, I would now take time to analyse my state of mind at that moment but somehow it was simpler than that. Victoria had done a massive amount of detective work and, by using just a few hundred pounds, we would know once and for all whether there was anything in the idea. And we would still have the bulk of the inheritance if there were no castles to be had in Italy.

I couldn't go as work kept me in London but Victoria asked her sister, Rachel, to go with her. Rachel spoke Italian, with a broad Roman accent it turned out, thanks to a year in the Eternal City as an English nanny just after she had left school.

It's a journey I have always envied them. Flying into Pisa, hiring the smallest Fiat and pushing off into what was for both of them the unknown. They stayed in some of the cheapest hotels and saw endless houses and villas by day, eating usually at long tables in the evening with the other assorted guests in the local trattoria. They travelled down to Lucca, but the houses there – even the most broken down – were too expensive. They then went on over the mountains to Città di Castello, 'a gloomy place' said Victoria.

Not one whit discouraged, the intrepid househunting sisters pushed on. They took the three-hour or so drive from Città di Castello, down the motorway towards Perugia, and then across country round Lake Trasimeno, to Castiglione del Lago, a walled town which juts out into the lake, the largest lake in the Italian peninsula. There Victoria, already smitten by the area, and most of all by the lake, met a man who was to dominate our lives for the next few years, the beguiling, annoying, irritating, generous, helpful and at times inspired Giancarlo Caponeri.

Giancarlo is a local man, who then lived with his mother, like so many 40-year-old single Italian males. We heard subsequently that he had been married once, but the marriage, for whatever reason, was no more. He worked in a bank by day in Perugia. The sort of job many Italians would kill for: it is safe, secure, pensionable and has some status. But Giancarlo, when we got to know him better, told us the bank was suffocating him. Giancarlo only stayed in the bank because his mother thought it was too risky to get involved in the property business full time. So Giancarlo conducted most of his estate-agency work either early in the morning or in the evening. Which explained one of his more exasperating habits: he was perpetually running late and was uncontactable during the day. The best time to see him was at weekends, when he would try to fit you in with all the other potential clients London was sending him.

Giancarlo Caponeri is of average height. And despite his name never wears a hat of any colour. His hair is brown, eyes brown, and his face usually smiling, even when he gets rather frustrated with women like Victoria who think they might know more about buying a kitchen sink than he does. His English is very good, idiomatic, and he seems to have a special liking for his British clients, of whom there are now dozens. He's a stickler for detail and, once a project is started, he makes sure that *you* know every detail. He is, in a word, punctilious.

We were lucky in finding Giancarlo, though there were times when we thought otherwise, particularly when he didn't turn up, or kept us waiting for two hours one Saturday morning. But those are merely irritating habits. Giancarlo was absolutely honest. In our innocence, we had not even thought of the possibility of dealing with rogues in Italy. I suppose, looking back, it was naïve in the extreme. A couple of summers later we met the author, Barry Unsworth, who had had the most awful time with some agents who had not acted in his best interests. He wrote a long piece for the *Observer* in London about it, warning the by then growing numbers of potential property seekers of the pitfalls.

Of course, I should have paid more attention to the background reading. One of the best travel books, though the least useful for my purposes, was written by Tobias Smollett, the man Laurence Sterne nicknamed Dr Smelfungus, because of his irascibility and hatred of foreigners. There's a marvellous incident in his *Travels through France and Italy*, written in 1766, about a hostler just outside Florence who put two untrained horses in the traces of his coach, and they had bucked and turned the coach over. Smollett complained to the authorities but they fobbed him off with a vague excuse.

Smollett goes on, 'In passing through the street to the coach, I met the hostler, and would have heartily caned him but perceiving my intention he took to his heels and vanished.'

The idea that Italians aren't to be trusted is almost as old as Italian history. Even Napoleon Bonaparte, no mean robber himself when it came to art treasures, is supposed to have said to an Italian lady *'Gli Italiani tutti ladroni.'* (The Italians are all robbers.) She is said to have replied, *'Non tutti, ma buona parte.'* In Italian a nice play on words, but the literal translation means 'not all, but a good part.' And in our own era, the most famous and numerous were the *tangenti* of Milan, the rip-off merchants who brought about the end of the First Italian Republic (loosely translated *tangenti* means bribe takers). World-weary Italian friends used to remark that they could understand a little skulduggery, that was normal in life, but these people became greedy and that was unforgivable.

And yet, do Italians really deserve such a reputation any more than any other nationality? In more than five years in the country we have never had a moment's anxiety. Nor had we a moment's worry with Giancarlo nor any of the people who gathered around him or who worked on the house which we subsequently bought. But I'm getting a little ahead of the story. First we had to find the house.

Having located the general area and a few possibilities, it was my turn for a trip. On that first visit of mine, Victoria and I were given a room at the back of the Hotel Miralago, in the main square of Castiglione del Lago and opposite the newly restored clock tower, whose chimes on the hour could be heard for miles. We had a marvellous view over the lake. It soon became 'our room' and, with the arrogance of regular clients, we always asked for it. On the few occasions that it was taken, we were suitably annoyed, and huffed and puffed to ourselves. Oh, the knee-jerk arrogance of the British traveller! Even after the fall of empire and the nation's shrunken role in the world, we still too often regard ourselves as superior to those who have been unfortunate enough to have been born into another culture.

Giancarlo turned up two hours late for my first meeting and Victoria's defence was beginning to wear rather thin, when he appeared in the Square, sweating in the Saturday morning spring sunshine but at least he had some news.

With virtually no time for any of the most basic of courtesies, he announced, 'I think I've found the house for you, it's the right price, a good position, and has marvellous views.' He packed us into his small diesel-fuelled Fiat, and we bumped our way out of Castiglione, along the straight piece of road towards Chiusi, before we turned off and started climbing the gentle slopes on the far side of the valley.

That morning, as we drove, I had my first view of the area that Victoria had said was the place for our new life. I remember cypress trees, most of all, jutting up tall and proud from the land, defining boundaries to some houses now derelict, to others still lived in. The houses were usually sited on top of a small hill or incline, so that they could be seen from a great distance, and were surrounded by cypress trees and shady pines. In one case these provided a grand entrance to a house on the lake shore where the owner had planted pine and cypress alternately on either side of a dusty driveway at least fifty years ago.

There were olive groves, some mature with the trees' thick trunks suggesting at least a century's growth, others more slender saplings, but all with their green and silver leaves moving in the slight breeze. The lines of vine were still dark branches growing along the supporting wires between sturdy concrete posts. But mostly it was green at that time of the year, with the winter's rains still keeping the roots refreshed.

And above, what else could there be but the blue sky, almost white on the horizon, turning to a deep satisfying blue the farther up into the sky you looked.

In the fields, all ploughed and planted now, water was being sprayed on the young crops from hoses, lifting the silver jetstream high into the air, so that it fell like a fine mist over the earth. And, in some places, the water spray was a prism through which the primary colours appeared in the form of rainbows.

I've learned that these are not rare days in Italy, to be treasured like a perfect summer's day in England, but happen day after day, until the heat of summer begins to give the land another look, of browns and yellows. No wonder the Italian for spring is *primavera*, the first green. I understand now what Dr Johnson meant when he said, 'A man who has not seen Italy is always conscious of an inferiority; from his not having seen what a man is expected to see. The grand object of travelling is to see the shores of the Mediterranean.' I would not have believed that one would remember such quotes from one's schooldays, nor that the first sight of Italy would conjure so many images that had been absorbed in art and literature down the years. But . . . I was becoming a literary cliché. In short, I was hooked.

As we left the main road between Castiglione and Chiusi, and turned up towards a place called Canta Gallina, a name that has been on maps in this region since medieval times, but is in truth no more than three farmhouses clustered together either side of a dirt track, the aspect of the landscape changed gently. From the height of the hills you looked out over a vast area of land to the west, rolling countryside, a lake, Lake Chiusi, in the distance, and Chiusi itself, like so many former Etruscan cities, built atop an easily defended hill. And in the distance, farther west, in what would soon become Tuscany,

Monte Amiata, the highest mountain hereabouts, snow-capped in winter and a place to go skiing. I was looking with the eyes of a would-be lover, seeing what I wanted to see, filtering out any blemishes on the object of my desire, like the flour mill which belongs to the local co-operative, the small cement works and a host of other small enterprises that make every region of Italy self-supporting.

In vain, I searched for white oxen pulling ploughs, as the journalist Michael Adams had seen when he first came to Umbria just after the Second World War to convalesce. He bought a house to which he retreated regularly after foreign assignments for the *Guardian* and other papers. I had read his book, *Umbria*, on the way out, knowing nothing about the region, never even having really heard the name until that article in the *Telegraph* had caught my eye. In fact, I knew very little of Italy at all. I had been there on a few assignments, to Rome a couple of times, and Milan, and once had a memorable weekend at a round table for economic correspondents in Milan organized by that doyen of Italian correspondents in London, Paulo Filo delle Torre.

Adams's book was a marvellous scene-setter for a newcomer to Italy and to Umbria. 'A quarter of a century has passed,' he wrote in the Preface to the 1988 edition, 'since I came by chance to Umbria and was captivated, not only by the beauty of its mountains and valleys, or the charm of the little hill towns which nestle between them, but by something intangible in the atmosphere, a sense of poetry, inarticulate but unmistakable, which seemed proof against the onset of materialism in the outside world.'

What a deliciously inviting thought that is. Of course, there are other arguments. This observation was made by Luigi Barzini in *The Italians*, his warts-and-all portrait of his homeland: 'Many foreigners clearly want to withdraw from the rude turmoil of active life, to preserve and cherish a romantic illusion about themselves, their excellent taste, genius, beauty, and rank, which could only be shattered by unkind confrontations in their own country. They pathetically want not to be contradicted by the facts.' So there you have it, two perspectives on a life for foreigners in Italy in general and Umbria in particular.

Both writers are correct. The two views don't contradict but reinforce each other. There is poetry in the Italian way of life, but there is also public display hiding private squalor. There is the danger that the foreigner will fall in love with the externals, the palaces, the churches, the frescos, the food and the wine and not see the substance of a people who have for thousands of years slowly acquired the lessons that make life tolerable, a life where, paradoxically, the possibility of political upset, violence and mayhem are all too common. The Englishman lives in a community that he believes he can trust and which is honest. The Italian lives in a community where he knows that he can only trust himself and his family.

Umbria is about as far removed from the demands of life in a city like Rome or London as you can get. It was, I knew instinctively, the perfect antidote to the pressures of my professional life. But in planning to go there, I didn't feel that I was abdicating, or opting out. Neither did Victoria. We had been together since my wife's death. Together we had completed John and Natasha's schooling and university careers. She had seen them through 'O' and 'A' levels, and degree exam nerves. But Victoria is a woman who likes to be challenged and stretched. She had been the director of a London estate agency – and the chance to oversee the renovation of a foreign ruin, learn a new language, was just what she wanted. Redheads are never idle.

The move would be a challenge. I saw then, I'm happy to

say, what I still see, a part of Europe that keeps in touch with the past, while not rejecting the future, that combines the best of both and avoids the worst. What I also knew as the three of us bumped along the metalled road over the ridge of low hills, was that Victoria was right – this was the place we could be happy in. If only we could find the right house at the right price . . .

The house Giancarlo had in mind was almost perfect, its near perfection enhanced by a blissful spring morning, the hedgerows crammed with the yellows and blue and whites of the wild flowers, the birds singing, the heat beginning to build but not oppressively so. The surrounding countryside looked at its very best. As far as the eye could see, on all four sides, fields of olive and vine were interspersed with small copses of Italian oak – small gnarled trees, which grow wild, only rarely achieving any sort of distinction, being used by the locals as a source of free tinder for their fires in winter. There was also an horizon, something that we, a pair of Londoners, rarely glimpsed in the city.

The house was of the right size, too, standing within its own few hectares for at least a hundred years. Although now deserted, when Giancarlo unlocked the chains that kept the front door shut and we went up a narrow flight of stone stairs, the first floor was still sparsely furnished. The owners had left everything of the old way of life: a simple table in the middle of the main room in front of a largish fireplace, with the surrounding bricks on each side and under the mantelpiece thick with black soot and smoke; on the table a piece of plastic cloth, yellow with blue flowers, and a couple of handmade chairs, with straight backs.

In the bedrooms, wardrobes were made of pine or poplar, with wooden latches to keep the double-fronted doors shut. The bed had been stripped, but the wrought iron bedhead remained, now rusted by the damp that had invaded the house during the winter months when it had been empty. The only pictures on the walls were the sort you buy near the doors of Catholic churches all over the world. I remembered these devotional images from my schooldays at St Peter's and Paul's in Wolverhampton, given as prizes by the nuns if we were especially good. On the walls in this house there was Christ, in all his splendour, and Mary the Mother of God, and another picture of a saint, possibly St Francis of Assisi. All of them were stuck on the walls without frames of any sort.

Half-way up the plastered walls, rough plaster I remember, the owners had painted a pale blue surround, leaving the rest white, though yellowing in a few places, giving the effect of a dado rail. The ceiling was of beams, with terracotta tiles in between. In one room there was a sink but no tap, the woman of the house having to carry water up those stairs in the red plastic bucket that stood underneath the sink between the two brick-built supports, from the well in the garden at the side of the house. There were electric lights, but the wires hung loose in places from the beams of chestnut where they had been tacked up. The house was a museum of the life that most peasants lived in Umbria until quite recently . . . an unremitting struggle on the land, with little to distract when work was done.

We looked over the place in that hurried kind of manner adopted by most would-be house buyers . . . embarrassed to be invading another's private space and poking about in other people's lives. Giancarlo took us out on to a flat roof of a shed which had been added much later, alongside the main bedroom at one end of the house. The garden was overgrown with brambles, and somewhere in there was the well. As we talked, a woman appeared at the gate to the property about twenty yards away. I say gate, but it was in fact two rather ancient gateposts, the actual gates having long since been removed. The woman, broad-bosomed, short and dressed in dark colours, stood and just stared. We stared back, but she didn't move. A few seconds passed, then she turned and walked away. Imagination wanted her to be the original owner, or even the farmer's wife who had rented the house and worked the land, come to see who might be buying what had once been her home.

We went on talking about what was needed: a new roof, the walls replastered, electricity properly wired. The list got longer and longer, even though the basic price, under £15,000, would buy us a fair amount of land and a sizeable house. We hummed and hawed and after another quick look round, drove back to Castiglione del Lago to, as we told Giancarlo, 'think about it'. In our hearts we thought we had found what we were looking for.

There is a protection for buyer and seller in Italy when it comes to property. No gazumping here. Once an offer is made and accepted, then the deal must go through: neither side can get out of the deal unless they pay some kind of forfeit. No matter how long it takes for the lawyers, and the local authorities to do the paper work, register the change of owner and so on, the deal will stand. So you think long and hard about making any sort of offer.

We took lunch on the terrace of the Miralago, overlooking Lake Trasimeno. What a history this lake has . . . two hundred years before the birth of Christ Hannibal slaughtered 15,000 Roman legionaries and their commander, the Consul Flaminius in three hours one misty morning. A sudden storm in the lake a few centuries later almost capsized the boat carrying St Francis of Assisi across the water. But for us, all was calm. There was a light heat haze over the water so you could not see the other bank twenty miles away, but we could just make out one of the three islands in the lake, Maggiore, Minore and Polvese.

We chose a fish from the lake, grilled and served with some spinach cooked with those tasty Italian bacon chunks called *pancetta*, with just a hint of garlic. Fresh fruit to follow. We had the place to ourselves. The problem with spring in Italy is that the season is so attractive, you are almost always in a good mood. The danger is that you want so badly to be a part of this idyll.

Do we, don't we buy the house? A marvellous position, we both agreed, but the work of restoring it would be enormous. We knew we would have to do work but until we had actually found, we had not realized how much work. Between mouthfuls, over the last of the wine, Colli del Trasimeno (from the hills of Trasimeno) and more coffee, the pros and cons were debated. The only decision taken was to go and have another look at the house before making up our minds.

We got lost, at first, along these largely unmarked roads which wind up hill and down dale, sometimes metalled, sometimes dust tracks. To the untutored eye one olive grove looks much like another and for townspeople like us, the lie of the land, all trees and vegetation, seemed to have no particular distinguishing marks. But eventually we happened on the right road and, as we approached the house this time from behind, going down a slight incline, we saw again its marvellous position, surrounded by views, with only one other house anywhere near it.

We didn't have the keys, so we could not go in, but we walked round it and sat on a stone slab, which had been put there as a seat under a rare giant Italian oak. As we sat, the woman we had seen that morning came once again to the gateposts and stood and looked at us. We sat and looked back.

Was she the mad woman of Canta Galina? Did she go round staring at strangers all the time? After what seemed like many minutes she started to walk up the path towards us and, as she got nearer, she smiled. Then our Italian was, to say the least, basic. But when she asked if we were English, we said *si* with enough conviction.

We discovered with words half shouted for us to better understand, and repeated, and lots of sign language, that she was living in the other house. She told us that this farm and house belonged to her, and that she was the seller. Would we like to come next door, out of the sun and drink a glass with her and meet her family? It was churlish to refuse.

Her house was much bigger than it had seemed at first sight from the road. The tall trees around it, which gave it a lot of shade, also made it seem more compact. In fact, it was very much what's called a *podere*, a huge farmhouse, with many rooms, and built on three floors.

Inside, the main reception room was simply but well furnished with lots of solidly made furniture of chestnut or walnut and all polished so you could see your face in it. It looked as if it had been in the family for generations. In the centre stood a massive table, its four legs thick and intricately carved. In the centre of the table was a bottle of wine and some glasses on a silver tray, already set out as if we had been expected to call.

As we sat down, in came three beautiful young women, dressed in skimpy swimsuits still wet from the pool at the back of the house. None, I would guess was out of her teens. They were typical young Italian women, beautiful to look at, coquettish but modest, or at least as modest as you can be in a scanty swimsuit sitting taking wine with a couple of complete strangers. The daughters of the house said little, and only seemed interested when I said we had a son, John, who was about their age. The fact that I had a daughter, Natasha, was of no interest whatsoever.

It was idle chat to no great purpose, until we made to go, because of the time. As we left the house, the lady said she hoped we would buy her house, because it had been empty for a long time, but it was a good house and a lucky one. And, she added, as a final clincher, 'it would be so good to have such nice neighbours.'

We were being gently sold, and I think at that moment, we were on the verge of saying 'yes'. Our rented car had been parked at the other house and when we went back we were suddenly aware of people at the far end of the building, of dogs barking and chickens running about. There was noise, and commotion. It was a very Italian kind of noise, animated cacophony that after a few years in the country you become used to but then it assaulted our delicate English ears, so used to people tending to whisper rather than shout in public.

Had we not had that glass of wine, we might never have discovered until it was too late that, at the far end of the house, there were separate quarters lived in by tenants who worked some of the land: the very poorest of people in the social scale, owning little but the clothes they had, their animals, and a few sticks of furniture. Today there are very few who still live in this way: they are a relic of a bygone age. We almost had the last remaining survivors of this share-cropping system as our next-door neighbours.

We knew that, given all that was good about the place, all that was attractive, there was no way that we would want to invest in a semi-detached house in central Italy. It would shatter too rudely the illusions we had about the life we wanted south of the Alps. We shared with Goethe the dream of living, 'where the lemon trees bloom, where the gold orange glows in the deep thicket's gloom, where the wind ever soft from blue heaven blows, and the groves are of laurel and myrtle and rose.'

Did the lady with the three daughters hide her peasants from us during our early visits, I wonder? Or were we blinded by our fantasy of Italy as we looked for a place to call our own?

Over the next two days, we looked with much more care at what Giancarlo patiently showed us . . . but nothing quite matched the first house we saw, even those that had no tenants living anywhere near the premises. Some were too big, some too small, some too far away, some too close to people. We had suddenly become very picky.

It was a frustrating week to say the least but, on the last day, Giancarlo called us unexpectedly to say he had found one last house, more or less in our price range. Did we want to see it?

Needless to say we were loath to be frustrated yet again but . . . why not? First Giancarlo got lost, which did not improve our mood of pessimism. What's more, the first glimpse we had of the house as we rounded a sharp bend on the dirt track was not that inspiring. It was a complete ruin all overgrown with brambles. The roof had almost fallen in, and Giancarlo warned us against going inside, or up what remained of the steps to the loggia on the first floor in case they gave way under, as he put it tactfully looking at me, 'our weight'.

It was not all bad, though, we found as we circled it warily. The house was set in a good position, with only one other building in sight. You had views over the surrounding country-side, to the east, the small town of Chiusi on its hill; to the west, up the rest of the gentle slopes to the wild woods which went over the slopes and disappeared from view. There were fields of olive and vine to the front of the house and an old olive grove behind it. There was peace and quiet, with only the sound of a cuckoo repeating its call. There was even more work to do than on the first house and this one was more expensive. But the shape and the situation swept away all inhibitions. This was the house.

I still wonder whether we should have looked some more, or come back a few weeks later and looked around again. But time was short: we had barely one day left of the trip. It was the most impulsive decision I've ever taken. We've learned since of people who have bought on impulse, only to regret it later. There was an antique dealer from Dover, I remember someone telling me, who sold up, came to Umbria and did up his house, only to go broke because he had not calculated how much money he would need.

I'm glad I didn't know about the dealer from Dover when we bought. Did he do what we then did when he took his decision? We decided to drive back and view it by moonlight. Even today, five years on, when the moon is full, we revel in the view from the house. The little lights of Chiusi in the distance twinkle like diamonds scattered on a dark velvet cushion. At dusk, as the huge, blood-red sun sets behind the mountains, a deep, deep orange glow remains for a long time. The dirt road, white in the moonlight, snakes up the hill and small animals rustle in the woods which cover the hillside just above us. A house, you might say, well met – and bought – by moonlight. A house we bought for our midsummer night's dream.

Just to make sure, we got up very early the next day and drove up there again, to see the morning mists in the valleys between the trees and hear the birds singing their hearts out. Even then, though the house was overgrown with brambles and weeds, we knew that we had found what we thought we were looking for, and just before our time ran out.

2 The Valley of the Fireflies

OUR HOUSE IS half-way up one of the slopes above the village. Approached by a long, winding dirt track, a classic 'white road' as they are called in Italy, it is muddy in winter when it rains and bone dry and dusty in the summer when it's hot. And the surface is bumpy any time of the year, given the rocks and boulders which come to the surface the more it is used.

Sometimes the dirt tracks in this part of Italy remind me of when I was very young and used to go and spend the summers with my paternal grandmother in Malvern, in a small cottage in the Wych cutting, where a road had been sliced through the Malvern hills. Umbria too, at times, reminds me of the Worcestershire of my early youth . . . gentle rolling countryside with equally gentle hills.

In Umbria, though, the dirt road serves more than one

purpose for it acts as a defence against unwanted visitors, since few can find it unless they know it. For that reason it is also a problem: getting a piece of furniture delivered, and a hundred other items which are needed when you are restoring property, soon strip the white road of its romance. Until we put the phone in, we used to rendezvous with delivery trucks and vans at a small bar in the village.

A dust track it may be, but it has a name . . . and a long one. In Italian it sounds quite stylish: *Via Voc val di lucciole*. Loosely translated, that becomes 'the road in the vicinity of the Valley of the Fireflies'. And at some seasons, in the gloaming, you can see the little creatures sparkle as they busily fly here and there among the trees and shrubs. We thought of naming the house Casa Lucciole, the house of the fireflies, until someone pointed out that *lucciola* is also a slang name for a street girl. It would have been the equivalent of calling the place, the 'House of Tarts'.

When the house was built, no one could say for sure. Leonardo Pascale, the broad-beamed builder from Calabria, who restored it for us and became a firm friend in spite of the often tetchy relationship between client and builder, reckoned that the original single room at the western end of the house, the portion with doubly reinforced sloping walls, was at least two hundred years old, most of the rest being added on in the later part of the nineteenth century. But then Leonardo may just have said that to please us, knowing the British obsession with history. Giancarlo, the agent, was less sure about it, but still claimed that it was mostly over a hundred years old. Our neighbours, slightly further up the hill, the Mancinis, said it was nearer 1880, when their grandparents first built their house. What usually happens in these places is that rooms get added over the years but, as far as we could discover, it was not until about the 1950s that the later parts of the house provide any actual evidence of the date. We've a couple of hefty stones in the walls, which have a name and a year scratched uncertainly on them.

The final addition was a most unattractive single-storey garage-like structure at the eastern end of the house. It has a sloping roof and is cemented to the former main exterior wall. Its original purpose was to store the feed for the animals which lived next door. The owners had punched a hole through the wall, so that the straw could be pitchforked through from one part to the other. Today, that food store is our kitchen, and we've turned the hole in the wall into a doorway, but I suppose we've kept to the original idea, in that the food comes through the enlarged gap to feed us as we sit around a table in what was once an animal stall, and is now our dining-room.

The kitchen does not go the whole width of the house, because the last small section is a built-in oven for making bread, complete with its own little chimney. Despite our intention of using it, we have not tried it yet. Nor indeed can we until a pair of small iron doors are made for us by the blacksmith in the village of Panicarola, Domenico Seghini, he of the dark eyes and the dashing moustache, who looks more like an actor in the Marcello Mastroianni mould, than a man who beats metal into wonderful shapes every day. It was Seghini who showed me how treacherous the language can be, when he rang and said that he was Fabro Cancelli. It was not a name I recognized, and the line was so bad he sounded as if he was calling from the southern-most tip of Italy. It's not unusual to have stray calls from complete strangers who always think you are in the wrong house, not that they could have misdialled. 'I don't know a Fabro Cancelli,' I said. 'Cancelli, Cancelli,' he repeated over and over again. 'Had he got the right number?' I insisted, 'My name is Hobday . . .' At that point he said his name was Seghini . . . Fabro Cancelli actually means 'I make wrought iron'. Names were always, and still can be, a terrible trap for the linguistically challenged. After all, our agent's family name is Caponeri, which means 'black hat', so why can't another man have the name 'wrought iron'?

However you translate it, there's no mistaking the family name of the previous owners, Gambacorta. It means 'short leg', or 'cripple'. To make matters worse, my dictionary adds the word *scherz* in brackets before it translates. *Scherz* is short for *scherzoso*, meaning a teasing word. Maybe it was carrying that name through life that made the two sisters, from whom we bought the house, so difficult to deal with at a personal level. But they weren't poor, for the property which they were selling was part of several tracts of land they owned in the area. The house had been let to a tenant farmer who had had to put up with all the inconveniences of life at the most basic level. The Gambacortas had just sat at home and enjoyed what income they could derive from it.

The two sisters were both roughly my age. And although it must be said they were of less than average height, neither could be said to have particularly short legs. I got their details – names and dates of birth – from the formidable deed of sale, with its stamps, signatures, maps and a whole collection of official documents which covered 24 foolscap sides of paper.

The older of the two was Maria Grazia, described as a spinster. The Italian word is rather more attractive, it is simply *nubile*. Her younger sister, by two years, was called Marcella, whose marital status, or otherwise, is not given in the documents of sale. So perhaps she is *nubile* too. The fact that she kept the family name, did not mean that she had not been married. It's a paradox that in a country where most women still play the traditional homemaker role, and pretend that the man is boss, many keep their maiden names. There is a third person mentioned on the sale document, Eleonora

Corbacella, described as a widow and in her seventies when we bought. She was their widowed mother, who had also reverted to her family name. But Signora Corbacella did not seem to figure in any of the negotiations over land or house.

We never met the old lady during all the time that we were negotiating and, on the few occasions when we chanced upon the two Gambacorta sisters, there was little said, and they were not very forthcoming about the house, preferring to deal only with Giancarlo. All we could glean from Giancarlo, who also said they could be difficult to do business with, was they had inherited the house sometime in the 1960s. There had been a tenant farmer, more a share-cropper who had lived there but he had given up the house to move to a more comfortable council flat in another village fifteen miles or so away. Even though the house represented only income, it seems to have been a huge wrench for them to sell.

As absentee landladies, I sometimes wonder whether they ever knew what conditions their farm workers lived in: without any running water, no lavatory either inside or out, and only one huge fireplace to keep the building warm in the bitter winter months of January and February. And the windows would have rattled like anything when the cold and cutting wind they call the *Tramontana* came whistling down from the north. It was only later that we were told about the great harvest parties the tenants used to hold in the autumn, when Umbria looks its most luscious, when a wild boar roasted over a huge open fire and someone played an instrument while others danced. So it wasn't all work and no play. But there would always be much more of the former and precious little of the latter in their lives.

The house, as the previous occupants had lived in it, was a traditional farmhouse. The ground floor comprised the stalls for the animals or storerooms. The drinking troughs, made of wood were still there, as were the hitching posts where the oxen must have been tied overnight. I'm told by some of the older country people that the heat from the animals as they huddled downstairs permeated up through the terracotta tiled floors and added warmth in the winter. But the smell and the heat in the summer must have been unbearable.

The first floor was where the tenant family lived. Again the traditional layout included some steps from ground level up to a small loggia, or balcony jutting out from the centre of the building. The balcony led through a double door straight into the main room, which ran for the width of the house. This was the main living area, where the family cooked, ate and spent what leisure time they had. There was a vast fireplace, which would have been kept alight all winter, with the warmth spreading through the rest of the house. Off this room, four doors lead to rooms half the size, the bedrooms. There are still people who live in this way today in Umbria and, up countless dirt tracks, you'll find a family still sharing their homes with their animals, with chickens and dogs and cats running in and out. And living off the land, eating nothing but what the mainly clay soil and their hard labour, day in and day out, can produce. What's more, you may recall, we almost bought a house with such neighbours in one half of it.

The family who live part time just up the hill, the Mancini, have not yet fully modernized their house. They've put in a bathroom, but no central heating, and they have electricity, but only a small cooker to cater for them. We spent an afternoon with them one autumn day, with the fire on, all huddled round in the main room. When Signora Mancini showed us the rest of the house, the rooms were icy cold, just as my house in Wolverhampton was, I recall, after the war, when your front was toasted, but the tips of your ears had chilblains, and you woke up in the bedroom with ice on the inside of the window panes.

Before the central heating worked in our house, we tried to light the fire, but it was only when we left the windows open that the smoke would go up the chimney, otherwise it came back down and filled the room. Giancarlo says that because we have put in new windows and frames, which were properly fitted so that there are now no draughts, the open fire does not draw as it should. To date we have kept the open fireplace because it is so magnificent, but there's an endless debate as to whether we put in a stove or build the base up higher. David Willey, the BBC's former Rome correspondent who used to live in a similar type of house just outside Cortona on the other side of Lake Trasimeno, has built a kind of iron table, upon which he lights the fire, storing the wood underneath to keep it dry. In all the other houses I have seen, the fireplace is usually much more enclosed, because of the smoke problem. Luckily the central heating system was fixed and ready by the next visit two months later, so we've never used the fire since. But most Italian visitors have solutions . . . 'Raise the floor up to the chimney,' said one, 'Build out the walls much farther,' said another, or 'Put in a new fireplace altogether.'

We've kept our own counsel and the fireplace, and we plan to get it working. One day I would dearly love to imitate another of our neighbours, Giovanni Filipini, who lives in an old house on a nearby hill. He toasts his fresh new bread in front of his fire, and then makes that delicious *bruschetta* – toasted bread, rubbed with garlic and a hint of olive oil, tasting slightly of the chestnut smoke from the fire. So far we've produced some olive oil, and we've started growing garlic. Once we get the small bread oven up and running and the fireplace working, we can make *bruschetta* with the best of them. But like all ambitions in Umbria, half the satisfaction is having them, for there is no rush to realize them. Time seems less pressing when you live with the rhythm of the seasons, even if you are only there for a few weeks at a time. There's always next time and it's something else to look forward to. Meanwhile, we have acquired some tenants who live in the chimney, some small bird has made its nest there and, as the days get warmer, we can hear its young chirping for food.

The roof, when we bought the place, did not really exist, only the beams and half the tiles were in evidence. The main beams were at least a foot square, balanced on supporting walls. The wood had been attacked by some kind of termite, but there is now a modern treatment that kills any such beast and protects the wood as well against further attack. They must have cut down some massive trees to get such beams. It's rare in Umbria these days that you come across wood growing tall enough to replace these supports. The beams were not only to keep the roof up. They had other uses. We kept coming across huge nails at various points for hanging hams and sausages or dried vegetables. The Gambacorta family or the farm worker had modernized in one respect, there was electricity but the wiring was a do-it-yourself job of the most primitive kind.

We had one stroke of good luck as we were in the process of buying the house . . . a process which can take some three months . . . in that the local authority had started to pipe water to the various houses outside the village. So, with a small increase in price to cover the cost of the work, we bought an uninhabitable house, but with electricity and mains water.

The land surrounding the house came right up to the foot of the walls. And on our first visits, we had to hack our way through undergrowth – brambles of the most spikey kind – to venture inside, and very gingerly, because not all the terracotta floor tiles were still in place. It was a scene of total desolation.

The great fireplace consisted of just the wooden surround of the mantelpiece, the chimney breast having collapsed. There were only two of the original internal doors left, the others looked as if they had been chopped up for firewood by some person or persons who had camped there for a time. All but three of the windows had been bricked up . . . not because of a window tax, as in eighteenth-century Britain, but because it was often the best way to keep the place warm in winter. So each bedroom had only one window, and even two of those were half bricked up. There were no shutters left nor any windows with glass, just the rather rotten frames.

What was revealed was just how tough life must have been for the people who lived on the land down the years: and writer after writer tells of the appalling conditions in which most of the peasants lived until quite recently. At one stage, the land surrounding Lake Trasimeno had been a malarial swamp. Most of the people were illiterate, rarely eating meat but a steady diet of seasonable vegetables, wine and bread. The startling historic truth is that it was ever thus, over thousands of years. Read, for example, Virgil's poem 'Moretum' about Simylus, 'the rustic tiller of a meagre farm'. Through the centuries foreign travellers have noticed the grinding poverty of the Italian peasant, left to rot by absentee owners. From Smollett in the eighteenth century to D.H. Lawrence in the early twentieth, the traveller in Italy talks of the poverty. Now it's become something of a modern literary genre in Italy, with writers like Italo Calvino, in *The Road to San Giovanni*, or Rosetta Loy, in *The Dust Roads of Monferrato*, describing the peasants' difficulties.

Such memories are at odds with the modern British dream of a home under the sunlit Mediterranean sky. Life is real and earnest, regardless of climate and vegetation. Take the example of one Englishman I met, who was so determined to realize that dream in the 1950s that on a whim he bought a house in Umbria. A real pioneer. Despite all his hard work and ingenuity, however, the challenge defeated him and he's now back home in Lincoln, a healthy eighty-year-old who does not regret for one minute what he tried to do, only that he failed to succeed.

He recalls trying to save rain in winter, in a complicated system of pipes and barrels, so that he could water his crop through the summer. No matter how much he packed every nook and crevice with old rags or paper, the wind, the *Tramontana*, when it blew from the north over the mountains, would get in. The fire was kept going all winter, if the wood he spent most of the summer chopping up, lasted. And in the dry summer months he would work from sun-up to sunset on his patch of land, keeping out the wild boar and other animals from using his cottage garden as their private store. He did not leave his hill for days, even weeks at a time. His light was candles or, later on, an oil lamp. And he remembers when the nights drew in, he'd look out from his vantage point over the valley towards Chiusi, with hardly any lights to be seen anywhere, with even those of Chiusi dim and scattered in the distance.

But he did not work entirely for nothing. When he was forced to retreat back to Britain, he kept the house. I know it well because it is perched on the hill more or less opposite my bedroom window and today it is home for his daughter Elizabeth and her husband Giovanni Filipini, who gave up their life in Rome for the quiet of the Umbrian countryside. Now there is electricity, a well and a small electric fence around the vegetable plots because the wild boar still come raiding at night when they think there is no one about. When John comes back from Lincoln in the summer, he still cannot believe that a way of life that had endured for centuries could change in such a few years. At the time he left, he could not have imagined the comfort and security that is now possible in these rough-built brick houses. Nor could the Umbrians, which is why they left them in their hundreds and moved into the towns and villages to live in *case popolari*, or council housing, provided by the Communist-Party-controlled town and village councils.

Given this history, a history of struggle and work, interspersed down the centuries by foreign invaders fighting over the land, the last time in 1944 and 1945, when many of these decent people were taken away by the Germans to be shot or sent to labour camps, it's little wonder that so many of them left their old homes and moved into the relative comfort of the council house, and turned to the supermarket to buy their food with their pensions.

When we bought the house, we knew nothing of this history. We knew nothing of Umbria, or its people. What we saw was a ruined farmhouse in a fine location with surrounding views over the countryside, woods, vineyards, olive groves. When we saw it in spring, the ground was covered with yellow dandelions, white daisies, purple heathers and the deep satisfying green of grass watered by the heavy morning dews of springtime. We could not understand why the local people still thought that we foreigners were fools to be parted from our money. They were, in the main, only too happy to be shot of the pile of bricks that they were not allowed to destroy but had to leave to time and nature.

Local politicians were operating a rudimentary environmental policy to preserve the traditional character of the countryside – even if it meant ruins on the one hand, and council housing in the shape of blocks of flats on the other. The locals didn't seem to mind leaving the old houses. To keep the land was much more important; an Italian peasant and his land are very rarely parted. But the house was another matter entirely.

It was just a pile of stones that had outlived its time. There was no need for sentiment there, when it fell down.

To us, with our plans to recreate an Italian dream, the house seemed a snip at £20,000, half my inheritance from my mother. To the sisters who owned it, the Gambacortas, it was 40 million Italian lire in the bank, and they could still keep the land and derive some income from that. At first they thought it was a miracle. But both sides in a way rushed in. I, for my part, should have been more careful about assessing its state. The restoration, as we euphemistically called the project (in actual fact, we should have just said rebuilding), quickly drained our resources and forced me to seek a bank loan, before we were anywhere near finished and able to live there. Looking back, I wished I had seen more clearly what would be involved. But then, should reality intrude on a dream? Should ambition be limited by common sense? Now that we've done it, I can answer a resounding 'No', but get me late at night, and with my defences down, and I'll tell you a different tale.

The Gambacorta sisters, too, regretted what they had done. Or, more specifically, the price at which they had sold. As we started to build, so the Gambacortas began to feel that they had been cheated. I'm told, by Leonardo our builder, that they used to drive over from their house in Sanfatucchio on Sundays and stand and shake their heads at what we were doing. And when after most of the rebuilding had been completed we had to agree the boundaries to the land with our two surveyors, Sergio Sargentini and their man, they stood out in the road, and barely spoke to us. They were dressed up to the nines for the occasion, hair freshly permed and tinted, smart clothes and city shoes. I tried to invite them in to see what we had done.

'It was our house, now it isn't,' said the elder half, looking

35

at her sister as she spoke. 'It's not ours any more. It's . . .' and her voice just seemed to stop, but the look seemed to suggest that the rest of the sentence would have told me that we had ruined it. Then I thought they felt we had not respected what had gone into it, the lives that had been lived there, the births, the deaths, the generations. Now I think those tears were for the millions of lire they could have made by rebuilding and selling at a bigger profit. It is outsiders like me that get sentimental about country people. Country people, in whatever nation, have too hard a time staying ahead of the game to be sentimental about anything.

We have never seen the Gambacortas since. Sometimes, when Leonardo comes over for supper with his wife Nila and their football-mad son Mateo (tell me about Liverpoo, he once asked me, clipping the final 'l'), we hear that they ask what else we've done to the house. But when they hear that there's a lawn where corn used to grow, they never comment. Their land still surrounds us on three sides. The deal left them with an awkward-shaped plot and, since we moved here, the land has been left to grow wild, only being ploughed once a year. But I don't feel too sorry for them. They claim Setaside from the government under the European agricultural policy, so they still derive a small income from it.

One day, as the price of agricultural land falls in Europe, I might be able to afford to buy the extra three or four acres, half an acre of which is a deep gully of stunted turkey oaks and rampant brambles, with a small stream, so we are told, running at the bottom. Then I could claim some Setaside, which would pay towards Giulio Cerboni who helps us maintain our plot. But how do I approach them? Could they sell it to someone else, who might want to build on it? Possibly not, it is zoned as agricultural land. But the possibility is there – the revenge of the Gambacorta sisters. Perhaps they know how we feel and that it is enough for them as they get older to know that we will never forget that this was their land and that some of it still surrounds us, the foreigners who 'stole' their property at a knockdown price.

But that's all past, the actual reconstruction was a different challenge. I realize now that I should have kept a diary. For a man who would take the complete set of Pepys's *Diaries* with him were he ever to be set down on a desert island, I'm ashamed that I don't. So the stories of the reconstruction of the house do not follow one another in any set sequence. The memories now are mellow ones of little discoveries, rather than problems. The pain of financing the project is more than cured by what now exists. Like having your teeth out without anaesthetic, the relief from the abscess is immense.

You start of course with the plans. That's the easy bit. You have to have the plans properly and professionally drawn, to get permission from the local council, or commune, to do any work at all. Leonardo would not start to lift one brick until it was all approved. Some kind of policeman comes round and asks him for the necessary piece of paper. Heaven help him if he does not have it handy: we could be fined on the spot. Waiting for the plans to come through is very frustrating . . . it can take years. Perhaps God is an Englishman, for we managed it in months.

The plans were the most creative and vital element and Sergio Sargentini, our architect and surveyor, did us proud, creating some wonderful scale drawings. We liked them so much that we have them framed in all their simplicity, just to remind us of those innocent days, and they hang in our hallway leading to the two smaller bedrooms to this day.

It was really quite straightforward. Straightforward on paper, that it is. We indicated where we would put new dividing walls, a stone terrace round the property, the bathroom, the new windows and we talked about keeping the whole in the style in which it had been originally built. In many ways, I think it would have been cheaper to pull the whole place down and start from scratch with as much of the original material as was possible.

What we had not really reckoned with was the fragile and therefore dangerous state of the house. It had stood empty for some twenty years, at our estimate. Open to the elements, heat and cold, rain, damp and the ravages of time. That was why it was relatively cheap to buy. According to Sergio, it could fall down at any time. At first we thought he was being just a little too pessimistic. We realized he was serious when Victoria's friend, Belinda Randall, bravely ventured into what would become one of the two smaller bedrooms, only to step on a rotten cross beam which promptly gave way and she fell half-way through the floor. It was a miracle that she suffered nothing more than a badly grazed knee. Had she thought to sue us, she might have saved us a lot more money in the long run. But we still did not see it for the omen that it was: while it might look substantial enough, it was going to need a lot of work and expense to make sure it really was solid.

So the first job was to insert huge iron tie bars at strategic points to keep the walls in place, and then start to replace all the defective beams and cross beams and to dig out the foundations. It was nothing less than a complete rebuilding job. The frustration for us was that we were not there while much of this was going on. I had to be back in England earning the money to pay the bills which began to plop with alarming regularity through the letterbox in London. But Giancarlo kept us up to date with a regular weekly report.

Not for the first time since we came to Italy was I struck by the deep sense of historical continuity in the ways things are done in the country. What we got from Giancarlo was a list of items bought, amount of brickwork laid or piping acquired for the water system. By and large there was very little comment about anything. There were no value judgements, rather just entries in a ledger. At first we found this a little disconcerting, because we wanted to 'know' what was happening, how it looked, what shape was emerging, whether those old tiles fitted. It meant a lot of telephone calls, another unforeseen cost of trying to restore a house a thousand miles from home. Finally, I understood that what Giancarlo was doing was what had always been done. If you delve into the archives in Florence, or any city in Italy, you will come across the records, or *ricordanze*, which most Italians kept over the years and which, for people like Iris Origo in her book on the fourteenth-century Merchant of Prato, or the Renaissance historians, are an invaluable source of information about the lives of the past. We've kept our *ricordanze* too and no doubt some future historian will unearth them, and be able to follow, almost week by week, how some foreign resident rebuilt an old farmhouse in the 1980s.

Giancarlo's less than emotional bare-bones record of what Leonardo and his team were up to is fleshed out though by some of the photographs that were taken along the way. Giancarlo keeps a photographic record to show future clients how the restoration process works. Some show the detail of iron work, or beams, or the team at work . . . and it has to be said, at play. When the house was finished, Giancarlo stuck some of them on a piece of board and framed them: we see the house open to the sky, as the beams are being treated, and the chain and pulley system being used to lower the great slabs of tufo stone into place in the surrounding terrace.

And we see the parties they had to celebrate this or that stage of work completed. Everyone sitting at a table, a huge fire on which something is being cooked, washed down no doubt by Leonardo's robust red wine, barely a few months old. And the system worked a treat: with what was essentially a four-man team, the work took barely six months. They started in May, just after the sale went through and the permission was granted and we were able to spend our first night in the house – admittedly without windows for two days – by the end of August, when we braved the mosquitoes to sleep on the floor under some blankets in the master bedroom. I remember we whispered to each other at every sound, worrying that some wild animal was about to leap on us out of the dark, having crept up the half-finished staircase, after entering by way of the large gap in the wall which would eventually become the door into the dining-room.

Restoring a house may be expensive and frustrating, but it does provide little by little a network of contacts who will be with you for the rest of your life. And such is the way of life in rural Italy that you get to know families and other contacts, until you are as much a part of the local system as anyone born there. It's like a giant spider's web that first catches you, and then traps you, and no matter how much you struggle, you can't get free of it. They come and visit. You bump into them in the shops, in the street, in the bars. They talk about you behind your back, and about each other to you. They know how well your olives have done, and that you've had friends out from England. They hear you've tried that new restaurant at wherever it is.

Yet despite all this togetherness, and sense of community, each man is proudly self-employed. The Italian word for 'self-employed' says it all: it is *indipendente*. None the less, Italians work well as a team.

If ever you want to build a house in this part of Italy, these are the heroes you should talk to. Leonardo is the boss, of that there is no doubt. From Calabria, he's worked his way up the peninsula, on the roads, and other construction projects, finally settling near Chiusi, marrying a local girl and settling down. A fearsomely hard worker, he's still seen by some as an outsider. Indeed, the people from the south are seen by almost all other Italians as different. He comes from a tough environment, a violent one if some of the stories are to be believed. But as a friend he's loyal to a fault, a man you would trust with your life. Built like an ox, his dark skin is burned by the sun, making his smile all the whiter. For him, he says, working on these old houses is the best work he's ever done. It's more creative, more demanding, than just sticking a few modern bricks together with a bit of cement. And even though he's not from Umbria, he likes the idea that somehow he is saving some of its history for future generations.

Equally the rest of the team have their own definite characters. Nazereno, the plumber, is the boyo: married, but with a twinkle in his eye. Always game for a laugh, always ready to flirt just this side of good manners with Victoria. When Giancarlo and Leonardo inserted a terracotta brick into the wall above the doorway into the kitchen, stating that they had restored this house in 1989, Nazereno went off and got a brass plate, which he screwed to the wall of the wash house, where the central heating boiler, a washing machine and the spare water tank are installed. On the brass plate, he had had engraved simply: 'Nazereno Vecchini, Idraulico, 1989'. I don't think I ever saw Nazereno over these past few years anything but happy.

The quietest member of the team was Fabio Bernadini, the electrician. Fabio was shy and unmarried. He still lived at home, looked after by his mother who no doubt believed that no girl would be good enough for him, spoiling him and making him very choosy. Unlike a wife, his mother was no doubt more tolerant of his habit of staying up late at night in the bar in the centre of Castiglione del Lago with his cronies, talking rather than drinking. Fabio was forty something, the age where most of the women of his generation were married. He was teased unmercifully, and whenever Victoria had a female friend to stay, Giancarlo used to suggest we invite Fabio over. We all went to the Communist Party festival in Castiglione one year, Victoria and I with Nazereno, Giancarlo and Fabio. All the political parties held these festivals for a week or so at a time during August, offering a massive amount of subsidized food and drink, a few stalls for local businesses to display their wares, and the occasional party political speech before the nightly dancing started. The *Festa del Unità*, the festival of unity, as the Communists called theirs, was the biggest and the best. The party has now changed its name to the Democratic Party of the Left, but the festival is still as good. Throughout the whole evening, Giancarlo and Nazereno pointed out this or that woman and suggested to Fabio that she was his for the asking. As a joke it was repetitive, and not very amusing, but Fabio took it in good part. He was a good electrician but he had one design fault. He always used white, plastic-covered wire, so that when he ran a cable from the wall along a beam to a light socket, it drew attention to itself. To overcome this, he used to painstakingly paint the cables black. After three years he managed to find some black plastic-covered cable, and since then he has never looked back. Tall, slightly sad looking, Fabio finally found a wife in Naples where there is, so I am told, a steady supply of women looking for husbands. He now has a family, has put on just a little weight, and never goes out at night to talk to his friends in the terrace bar in Castiglione.

As in all such groups, there is a father figure. Older than the rest, Vittorio Coppeti is the carpenter. A true artist in wood, he made all the windows and doors and fixed them. Each one is bespoke, each fits perfectly, and all are fitted with those amazing hinges which are so common in Italy. In reality, they are metal hooks which fit into the wall and on which the door or window is hung. Given that no wall is perfectly straight or true, and that there are no such things as right angles when it comes to making door or window spaces, these hooks enable the doors to hang straight and true whatever the shape of the wall.

Vittorio is a grandfather, with grown-up daughters. He is immensely proud of them, and seems to spend most weekends eating at this house or that with the whole family. He lives over his carpenter's shop in the nearby village of Paciano. You hardly see the building, for the planks and logs piled high against the walls. Inside, it's dusty and full of sawdust, with some relatively modern machinery to cut, bend or glue the wood. It looks as if no one could ever find anything, that all measurements get lost as soon as they are noted down on the back of an envelope or an old bill. But Vittorio knows where everything is, and the doors and windows leave the shop on time and in the right order. He never fails.

Other people got involved from time to time in the project . . . there was the man who sandblasted the walls and ceiling tiles to get the brickwork back to its original, deep, satisfying fire-red colour. There was the man who treated the beams to kill off the termites and other insects who live in and off the wood. There was another man who treated the floors and another whose sole job was to apply the whitewash to the rough-plastered walls. There was another man whose job was to put in the septic tank and there was the man who installed the gas *bombola*, the huge white tank that provides the fuel to heat the house, the water, and work the cooking stove. There's a whole network of people, each known to the other, working in narrow trades but moving from house to house, project to project, all experts in their field and all, it seems, making a living. Sometimes it leads to confusion. Nazereno, our plumber, sub-contracted some of the work to Claudio, who shoots wedding videos on the side. Claudio looks after the electrics mainly – the thermostat, or the inner workings of the central heating boiler. We have never worked out who we call, because usually the one we call says it's the other's job and vice versa. Sometimes, I'm convinced, they agree in private who will do the job. No matter, it always gets done. Throughout the summer of 1989 these individuals flitted in and out, like bit players in an Italian soap opera. The four principal actors, though, were nearly always around, with Giancarlo Caponeri playing the part of the theatre director, improving performance where he could, chivvying, nagging and, in many ways, such was his interest, behaving as if it was his house not ours.

So much so, in fact, that on those occasions when Victoria would travel out to get up to date, they would have sharp tussles over which tile to put in the bathroom, or whether the kitchen would have this sort of working surface or that. At times Giancarlo, it has to be said, behaved like a spoilt only son and almost stamped his foot with impotent anger, until he remembered just in time that we were the clients. But he had one particular habit which proved very useful: he liked to show us other houses he had been involved with, and this gave us lots of ideas. The kitchen, for example, was the result of one such visit to a house owned by a Chinese surgeon from Hong Kong. He had put granite slabs on bricks to create the kitchen's working surface, with doors fitted between the small brick walls to form the cupboards. This prompted a visit to yet another tradesman whose name we never discovered and whom we call 'the marble man' for simplicity's sake. At first glance, and to an untutored eye, he looks like a baker covered from head to toe in a fine white dust, which looks like flour but is, in reality, the finest marble dust swirling around his grinding, polishing and sawing machines. The marble man has, in his yard, every shade of marble and granite you could wish for. The massive slabs lean one against the other and you just go and choose the sort you want. We chose a dark, ruddy-brown piece of granite, which is wonderfully cool in summer. But he has also made us a grey-grained granite shelf, and a virginal white marble tabletop for a bathroom. It's this that makes the restoration so interesting in Umbria: the trades are all still there and you know each man who made whatever it is personally. Like Domenico Seghini, who did the wrought-iron bars on the ground-floor windows, and the banister both on the external steps up to the loggia and the internal stairs up to the first floor. Made to measure and yet costing very little, relatively speaking.

It has to be said that without Giancarlo's guiding hand, we would never have managed it. Our only problem was some-times in getting hold of him. Giancarlo is the only true worka-holic I have ever met. When we got involved at first he was still working by day at a bank in Perugia, nearly thirty miles away. Since we were one of many clients, we had to exert the patience of Job.

It must be said in his defence that at that stage in the 1980s, the growth in the business of selling houses to foreigners was still in its infancy. Giancarlo had been involved in a desultory fashion for some years, as agent for a British firm in Yorkshire, Brian French and Associates. Mr French had sold out to the Yorkshireman of Victoria's first phone call, Steve Emmet, who had set up and improved the network of agents in Italy. Steve Emmet and Giancarlo were similar in one essential characteristic: they had an old-fashioned, honest and rather personal way of doing business. You felt they dealt with you because they liked you. But it meant that you got to know them rather better than most agents. Steve and his wife came to supper on more than one occasion, just as we ate out on any number of occasions with Giancarlo. This personal touch helped to smooth things over when, as clients, we felt that we were being given the runaround . . . not being able to get hold of Giancarlo, for example. But I must not exaggerate. Most of the time, indeed nearly all of the time, everything worked well but when every week another bill arrives for tiles, or cement, of another tranche of cash for the builder, the pain of spending needs the analgesic power of hospitality.

Giancarlo was also undergoing one of those moments in a man's life when a decision has to be taken. The bank job was safe and secure for life but he was beginning to see the future lay more in property. Steve Emmet, for his part, wanted more from Giancarlo because the demand for houses abroad was growing apace in the Thatcher years of plenty. How heady they seemed then, how brief they were in reality . . . remember the boom that was to set the British economy on a permanent growth path until the next century?

As more and more British would-be expatriates, not to forget the Germans and the Dutch, trekked south, so Giancarlo was getting to bed later and getting up earlier, to fit in all the visits, all the meetings, all the paperwork. That he did it at all was a miracle in itself. But the strain was such that he had to make the break and it was with a great sense of relief for all his clients and friends when he did. Giancarlo now has his own agency, Domus Italia, and his own office in the centre of Castiglione, in a beautifully restored building, where he has installed marvellous old furniture – a fine example of the work he is engaged in. He has also installed Anna Maria, whose English rivals his in fluency, to keep things ticking over as he prowls the countryside, checking on restorations in progress, and seeking more buildings and their owners to put on the market.

The end of the 1980s was something of a setback as Europe

moved into recession. From our point of view, it seemed to halt the drip, drip, drip of British immigration, so much so that we still feel able to claim that we know in the main only Italians in our part of Umbria. Nowadays Giancarlo deals with as many Italians as foreigners, as more and more leave the noise, dirt and crime of the big cities and come back to the Italian countryside. And the Italians too have discovered the joys of living in restored and modernized farmhouses. So much so that there is now even a very glossy monthly magazine devoted to the subject, plus any number of others on country living, cooking and gardening. From an investment point of view the only fly in the ointment was the state of the Italian lira . . . as long as it stays around 2,250 lire to the pound, I make a handsome profit if I sell. If the politicians of the Second Republic make a success of things and actually manage to govern the country to its full economic potential and the lira starts to get too strong against sterling, then I'm done for. My only hope is that British politicians can make a sufficient enough success of the British economy to keep the exchange rate on an even keel. Experience prompts me to believe that whatever party they belong to, the Italian or British, nothing much will change.

The currency equation is of some concern, but so far the movement over the five years has been plus or minus 15 per cent either side of the rate at which we bought. It's meant that sometimes we've benefited, as when we dug a well with the lira at its low point against sterling, and lost when we built a retaining wall. But if you work it out on what city analysts would call pound-cost averaging, then we are about even-steven over the five years.

In the end the house was finished and ready for habitation within about six months and we were able to celebrate with the team in the most unexpected fashion. More or less every year there is a foreign property fair in London where buyers, sellers and agents get together. Almost as soon as we had finished the house Giancarlo decided that he would take the core team to London to visit the show – at the Waldorf Hotel in London that year – and give them a few days' holiday. They paid for themselves, but Giancarlo and Anna Maria organized the flights, the hotels and the programme. When we heard about the scheme we invited them over to our small terraced North Kensington house for supper.

Leonardo, Nazereno, Vittorio and Fabio had not been out of Italy before, let alone on a plane. They were also out without their wives in London, so they were determined to savour as many of the delights as possible. Inevitably, they ended up in some dive in Soho; remember that none of them speaks a word of English. The story they tell of drinking beer and watching the show is hilarious. They could not believe such sights, or the offers that were made to them by the girls in the bar. But it was all good fun, until the bill was presented. It was massive. The way Nazereno tells it, they paid what they thought was the right price and started to leave. A bouncer barred their way. The bouncer had never been to Calabria. Leonardo, says Nazereno, just looked at him with a special Calabrian look, the look of a man who would use a knife if he had one, his hands or anything else if needs be. It was the look of a man brought up in the most violent part of Italy, where the mafia and 'ndrangheta are in control and where the vendetta is a way of life. The bouncer understood the look, and they left without a word. As I say, Leonardo is my friend but I would fear him as an enemy.

They were full of the story when they arrived at the house. Victoria and I had debated what to give them and had settled on shepherd's pie as the most traditional dish we could offer. Mind you, she put more herbs in it to satisfy the Italian taste buds. Everyone had second helpings and they had brought wine all the way from Umbria for the evening. It was strange, but fitting, to see the team in London in our kitchen tucking into English food with such gusto, talking of their triumph in the den of vice, asking for second helpings, and wiping the platters clean. But most of all, what I recall of that evening was when the team, who had provided us with such a beautifully restored house in Italy, cast their professional eyes over a property built by British craftsmen at the turn of the century. As all Italians, they were lavish in their praise.

'English electricians are very good ... look at that light fitting,' said Fabio peering underneath a kitchen cabinet where there's a small strip light.

'These are solid walls, really well built,' said Leonardo, tapping the exterior wall between the kitchen and the garden behind with his knuckles.

'I hadn't realized that British bathrooms were so modern,' said Nazereno, when he came downstairs, 'the lavatory flushes very quietly. That's good.'

'I'd heard that there were good carpenters in England,' said Vittorio, admiring some bookshelves in the sitting room.

And Anna Maria, not to be left out, said, 'Why do people joke about English cooking, it's marvellous.'

Only Giancarlo didn't say anything. He just smiled a contented smile, knowing that one more set of customers was happy.

3 Commanding Nature

NOTHING COULD BE in sharper contrast to our piece of land in Umbria than the small walled garden in North Kensington which is virtually maintenance free. By buying in Italy, without a moment's hesitation or any thought of the consequences, we went from the horticultural certainties of a tiny patch of rich, black earth in London to nearly two acres of pale, clay soil in the Valley of the Fireflies. And it was that part of the leap into the unknown which, as you will see, is why it was the land rather than the house that nearly defeated us in Umbria. Gardening, they say, is commanding nature. Sometimes I wonder who was commanding whom. It was, to say the least, a challenge, and a very steep learning curve if we were not to spend more than we could afford and still end up with nothing very much to show for it, except aching backs, broken hearts. Winston Churchill, like Garibaldi in Italy, offered the nation 'blood, sweat and tears'. He could well have been talking about the land and recalling one of his ancestors.

George Spencer Churchill, fifth Duke of Marlborough, spent his fortune creating the gardens and the palace of Blenheim. He also spent almost as much on books. The duke was, writes Mary Soames, '. . . foolish and extravagant, and dissipated the family fortune . . . he was an object of scorn or pity to his contemporaries . . .' Obviously the Hobday family is nowhere near the same league as the Marlborough family but all is relative and the house in Umbria was very much a scaled-down version of a Blenheim in my life.

I doubt I shall ever regret taking on a ruin in Umbria, but every time I bring out the photographs to bore another friend about the land in Italy, deep down I think they probably view me with pity . . . mixed I hope with just the right amount of envy. But then that is the fate of all enthusiasts. Yet before we started work on the house in Umbria, I would not have thought that I could be so carried away with the idea of developing a house and a garden in London let alone a thousand miles away in the centre of the Italian peninsula.

The garden in London had been created largely so that, apart from dead-heading the flowers and five minutes cutting the pocket-handkerchief lawn every week, very little had to be done. The acquisition of a camellia, by accident rather than design, and the mention of it on the *Today* programme, when there was a short interval before the weather forecast, won me the undeserved reputation of being a gardener. Mentioning the camellia, a fine plant I must say, produced some lively correspondence and even honorary membership of the International Camellia Society (whom God preserve). But, in my heart, I knew that, at that time at least, I was really sailing under false horticultural colours. While I liked gardens, well, liked looking at them, the thought of listening to 'Gardeners'

Question Time', even in its old and trusted format, produced a yawn. But the passing of years and the approach of retirement works on the subconscious in subtle ways, and getting to grips with a garden is one sure sign of trying to make what time we have left pass as slowly as possible. Everything moves at a slower pace on the land, so life seems longer. When you are in your fifties, that's a precious thought.

After grappling with two acres in Umbria, planting sixty olives, twenty other assorted trees, building a retaining wall, investing heavily in spades, rakes, a motorized lawnmower and spending many hours talking to the Margheriti Brothers, who own one of the largest garden centres in Italy, six hundred acres in and around Chiusi, I can now claim some experience. Knowledge, a little. Expertise? I doubt it, nature never lets you rest on your laurels and we've planted hundreds of them around the property, so that Victoria can justifiably call it, Casa del Lauro, Laurel House. We've also replanted them in some places where they never seem to take. We've watered and clipped them, sprayed them and nursed them. The laurels, they say, go to the victor. I am beginning to understand why they were so prized by the ancients: they take a great deal of time and energy, and a lot of patience before they become a massive laurel hedge, deep, dark green and shiny.

Laurels were once very symbolic: apart from crowning the victor (and young graduates on degree day in some Italian universities still wear a laurel wreath around their necks), the ancients believed that the laurel protected you against lightning. After jibbing at cutting the hedge and watering it in summer, once I knew this, I suddenly looked at the laurel hedge growing strong and forever green around the house in a new light and became as keen as Victoria to go on planting them around the edge of the land.

We're still buying laurel to fill gaps between trees. Back in those early days, those first few scrawny plants made little impact on the huge amount, huge to us at any rate, of land we had acquired. It was our own fault. After a great deal of haggling we managed to extend the original offer, of just the house and a small path around it, into a parcel of land of just under two acres.

The Gambacortas' surrounding land, however, becomes so dry in high summer that the weeds and grasses would be a fire hazard were they left to the mercies of the chain-smoking locals, who don't seem to have heard of the dangers of smoking. Victoria tends to follow Giulio Cerboni, the gardener, around the land with an ashtray to stop him tossing his smouldering butts here and there.

Given this bare earth, we started with a fairly simple plan: plant a few trees to provide a bit of shade in high summer and some shape to the landscape in the immediate vicinity of the house. We also wanted to preserve the look of the place as much as possible, as we had done inside the house, working, as we saw it, in sympathy with what had gone before. The first move we made, after the rush to put in the laurel, was to buy some trees: two cypress, two robinia, two pines and a tree, which looks a bit like a silver birch but isn't. It's a member of the acacia family. The pines and the cypresses are everywhere in Umbria and Tuscany; they are such a part of the local landscape that one cannot avoid planting them. The robinia were suggested by the Margheriti brothers, whom we stumbled across by chance. The brothers, Mario and Enzo, run one of the biggest garden centres in Italy, one near us, and a second down near Rome. You name the plant, they've got it somewhere under the acres of greenhousing, or they can get it for you. It was Mario, the burly, bearded brother in charge of the Chiusi branch of the family business, who suggested the robinia. They are not really trees in the true sense, but bushes grafted on to trunks, which quickly thicken out to provide shade. He also suggested the *pseudo accacia*, sometimes called the 'mophead acacia', to add variety. It has no flowers or thorns, unlike some of its cousins, and is still on the scrawny side five years on, despite some radical lopping. Mind you, we are not as brutal as the locals who will cut back so hard that all that remains is the trunk and some tiny twigs. It's vicious and they seem to do it every year.

When we started we bought what plants we liked the look of from the garden centre, had them delivered and planted. Now we are beginning to know the names and recognize the plants, I'm not so sure that it helps us amateurs. Whatever their names, Victoria and I argue a great deal of time about where to put them. It took us some time to appreciate the fact that nature has so designed trees that wheresoever you put them is right . . . though obviously some places are 'righter' than others.

The first plants we bought were a wisteria placed at one corner of the wooden pergola, and a vine at the other corner, each using the upright beam to climb, then spread over the horizontal beams to provide the summer shade. The wisteria proved to be the best investment because, within a year or so, it had more or less covered the pergola. Which meant that we sat under the pergola and watched the trees a few yards away stubbornly stay much as they had been on the day that the Margheriti Brothers' man, Marino, had first planted them for us.

Mind you, let's not be too hard on Marino, who has planted and grafted, and lopped and pruned, above and beyond the call of duty every time he arrives with another lot of plants. Always smiling, ever ready to share his knowledge with us or Giulio, who was at first, I think, a little wary of this stranger on his territory. Now, both seem to take as much pleasure in the place as we do, as if it was theirs, not ours.

While the wisteria went wild and grew like a mad thing year

on year, the great disappointment was that it never flowered, just went on producing leaves at a very fast rate. Once again it took us some time to get to the bottom of the problem but at first the shade it provided was more important than the flowers that would have given us a suitably picture-postcard look in springtime. Flowers were a low priority.

The vine moved more slowly but now, five or six years on, it is the vine that covers the pergola much more thoroughly and produces some marvellously juicy eating grapes at the end of the summer. It's only latterly, after experimenting with a wisteria in London, that we've learned how to prune it back to five shoots in summer from the trailers, and then back to two shoots or buds in December. I hope that the next summer will bring the first mass of pale blue flowers across the front of the loggia and up to the eaves, leaving space for the vine to go on growing. In fact, we have been so encouraged by the way the two plants have shot ahead that we've doubled the size of the pergola, extending it farther out from the house. Suddenly, it seems, when you've learned to prune and train such plants, the confidence to command nature increases at the same rate. By extending the pergola it means, once it is fully covered, that we have more shade during the day, even when the sun is at its highest and hottest in the middle of August.

But back to the trees. They were put in almost as soon as the house was finished, in 1989, and it was touch and go during the summer of 1990 as to whether they would survive. We used to try to water them with mains water but in summer the pressure is so low that barely a trickle emerged from the end of the bright red plastic hosepipe that Giulio brought up with him one day. We may not have liked the red plastic hosepipe but we liked Giulio's watering system, which is to dig a small, hollowed-out shape in the earth round the root, so that the water collects there before slowly sinking down to the roots. Inevitably, townees that we still were, and from a country where rain is more normal than not, we never gave the trees enough water. We would just fill up the hole and leave it at that. Our friend Ornella Contini, not only a memorable cook but a great gardener, told us to leave the hosepipe just trickling for hours so that the roots would be properly soaked.

As with everything we undertook, from shopping, cooking and almost all the household chores, our persistent questioning of friends and neighbours and, sometimes, even total strangers met on a walk somewhere, got us through those early days as complete novices in the art of gardening in general let alone in creating a garden in a foreign country. The problem was, though, that we did not always understand the answers. We have acquired a small vocabulary of the technical words used locally. For example, *vasca*, in the dictionary, is a small basin, but in gardening it's the small ditch you dig round a tree trunk to fill with water letting it soak slowly down to the roots. When we first came across the word, we rushed to the dictionary only to find that the authors of the huge Collins *Sansoni* knew many things, but were not thinking of gardeners when they compiled their masterwork.

But, by dint of sign language and practical demonstrations, we acquired the beginnings of the knowledge necessary to garden in a climate with hot summers and briefly cold winters. It has to be said, though, that the Italians love showing off their knowledge and sharing their expertise when it comes to such country pursuits as growing fruit and vegetables; and cooking the results for family and friends. Whereas in Britain the weather is the great conversation topic in company, in Italy food – its growth, its preparation and its consumption – is the essential standby for the visitor. Mind you, while they are willing to help, they leave you to make your own mistakes.

Victoria conceived the notion that we must have a lawn, or

at least a grassy area around the house. The advice we got from Giulio, who was happy to consider the possibility of not tending weeds for much longer, was that we should put some better topsoil down. To save money, never a good idea when it comes to gardening, we asked the local garden shop run by the bearded and jovial Signor Tosti, if he could supply us with a couple of lorry loads of good soil.

Our first mistake was going to Signor Tosti, the second was in being impatient when the soil did not turn up when we expected it. Let me explain. Mr Tosti himself is a fine man, helpful, respectful, willing but I don't think he is really an expert. We had gone to him because Giulio felt that ignoring him, a man in our own village, was somewhat insulting. You support your own in Italy . . . you are loyal to your own village. We were expected, therefore, to shop in the village, and not stray anywhere else. The Italian word which sums it all up is *campanilismo*, from *campanile*, or bell tower. So by buying those trees from the Margheriti Brothers (barely 15 kilometres away), we had spent money outside the community and that was not altogether the right way of going about things if you wished to integrate yourself into the village and become accepted. So to Signor Tosti we went to buy the topsoil and plant the seed. It was not an altogether altruistic move, it must be said. Tosti was cheaper and nearer and, if it worked, he was on the doorstep so to speak, so could provide us with help whenever we needed it.

Mr Tosti turned up at the house and together we walked round the area; he nodded and agreed with everything we said. He had the ingratiating smile of a professional salesman. Yes we needed topsoil, yes it was a good idea, and yes it would make our already beautiful house even more beautiful, and it would be something of an honour for him to help us create a garden. I've mentioned this before, the knack the Italians have of making you feel special, as they ladle out the compliments which you know you shouldn't believe, but inevitably you do. The Italians are experts, and they've been at it for years. Plutarch, in one of his essays, talks about the difference between friendship and flattery and how impossible it is to be an objective judge of yourself, which is what the flatterers work on, for they tell you what you want to hear in just the right doses. I don't know whether Mr Tosti had read Plutarch but Plutarch had Mr Tosti off to a T.

A deal was struck. Mr Tosti, assuring us of his own personal attention, got into his Fiat pickup truck and drove back down the hill to his small garden centre, which lies alongside the main road between Chiusi and Castiglione del Lago. It was not until the next time I drove past it, on the way to the bank in Castiglione, that I noticed that Signor Tosti's *vivaio*, or live-plant business, was in his wife Christina's name. I should have paid more attention: in a land where men still take first place, and women still pretend that men are in charge, putting the business in your wife's name must be significant.

At first we put the delay in getting the topsoil down to the fact that life moves at a slower pace in Umbria. Rarely do you get instant service. We waited, and waited and waited, and still no soil came. Finally, we phoned, and phoned and phoned, to be told politely, 'yes, it was on its way, but the rain had made the place muddy', so he was waiting until the weather calmed down a bit. After we had left for England, we got a call from Giulio to say that the soil had arrived, and was he to level it out. No, we said, that was Tosti's job. We came back on a flying visit, thanks to some unexpected air miles, and found that the torrential autumn rains that year had washed half the soil away. We set to and tried to level the rest as best we could. Over the winter more was washed away as rains lashed the hillside and, when the sun came out, as it does sometimes in January to suddenly warm everything up, the topsoil got blown away by the *Tramontana* whistling across the mountains in the north, bending the trees almost at right angles, so hard did it blow and so persistently. By spring, the soil we had bought barely covered the old rough earth that we had hoped to bury. Mr Tosti did not tell us that we should have sown the seed back in October, late maybe, but at least some of it would have taken root and held more of the soil in place. It was an expensive lesson and one we did not repeat when we came to lay down some more soil alongside the house to create a shady walk towards what had become an olive grove.

In those early years much of our gardening was of the two-paces-forward, three-paces-back variety. Wonderful ideas, which died with the heat or the lack of water, or were killed by the sudden frosts of February, like the mimosa that Giancarlo Caponeri gave us as a house-warming present when we moved in. Then there was the fig tree, which produced two figs in its first year, both taken by birds while still very small, and then resolutely refused to grow more than five leaves at a time on the end of each of its two scrawny branches. Or the hibiscus we planted so carefully near where we park the car, only to have some guests drive over them almost as soon as they flowered.

Giulio, uncomplainingly, cut down the weeds around the house with a small scythe that we bought in a moment of trying to identify with the local way of doing things. Scythes are very sharp and they do work well in long grass. They really slash through the undergrowth. But, after ten minutes or so, they soon lose their charm as a traditional gardening implement. We may have been right in our intention to buy a scythe but we had in fact bought a sickle, a small one, which meant you had to bend down low to cut the grass. We should have bought the bigger version, the two-handed job, which you can use while standing up relatively straight. For nearly a whole growing season Giulio would trim the weeds, bending down with the sun on his back, trying to make the weeds resemble some kind of grassy area near the house.

It was Giulio who suggested quietly that a strimmer might be a better idea. But again we made the mistake of buying one that was too small, and too fragile. 'Saving money only seems to cost more in the long run' is now our first law of gardening. If you can't afford it, don't do it. If you can afford it, do it properly. We thought we did have these handy rules in our minds, so we were quite proud of our first machine for the land. We unwrapped it as soon as we were out of the car, plugged it in and set to work on the grass . . . for about 30 seconds. The lights fused, so strimming for the next few weeks involved two of us. Me with the machine, and Victoria standing next to the main fuse box ready to push the fuse back in as soon as it popped out. And all the while we watered the trees by hand morning and night, day in and day out. Like Jean de Florette in that French film of the Marcel Pagnol classic, we were fighting a losing battle, and our neighbours did not want to interfere. There was a lot of sweat expended and not a few tears.

For once the publishing industry had let me down. As far as I could discover there were no books in English on gardening in Italy in particular, or the Mediterranean in general. Come to think of it, why should there be? There were some in Italian, but they were fanciful tomes, one of which started off, 'Get yourself a good gardener . . .' Well, we had Giulio Cerboni, who was respectful, and did largely as he was told, with a knowing smile, it must be said, as he indulged us in our fancies. Giulio is a resourceful man, and a demon worker. He arrives in his little three-wheel truck, puts on his little red hat, pulls on his blue overalls, dons his gardening boots and off he goes. Yet another contact of Giancarlo's, he has helped us through the worst and now enjoys what we hope is much better.

One of Giulio's most practical suggestions was that we buy terracotta pots and potted plants. As he pointed out, the soil is so bad in our area that everyone prefers to grow flowers, even herbs, in pots filled with good soil (*terriccio* in Italian). At first it seemed rather odd to have all that land around us, bare and empty, and grow things in pots as if we lived in a small flat with only a balcony. His suggestion was that we start with geraniums, those ubiquitous and colourful plants which adorn every window and doorway around the Mediterranean from Gibraltar to the toe of Italy. How right he was: even rank amateurs like us could not fail. These things just grow and grow, the more you pick, the more they sprout flowers, just a little water every day and you have a marvellous display. And the curious thing was that geraniums gave the place a much more Italian look than almost anything else we did in those first few years. People who live within the walls of Castiglione del Lago or Città della Pieve grow geraniums and, even in the narrowest and most shaded of streets, the reds and pinks make a huge splash of colour. There's one house in Castiglione, in whose walls there are rounded metal pot holders. A small plastic tube runs from pot to pot so that, by turning on the tap, the geraniums can be automatically watered no matter how far they are from the window or the small balcony. Mind you, woe betide you, if you happen to be strolling underneath at watering time.

We did not need any persuading and took Giulio's idea up immediately. At least we would have some flowers to show for a couple of years' part-time residence in Umbria. Success with geraniums bred ambition. Once again, though, it was more expense, as the profligate foreigners went on a pot-buying spree – round ones, big ones and small ones – and planted geraniums in all of them. Just a little water, every day, and the flowers kept coming. We ventured into hydrangeas, and more flowers. At least the house, surrounded by strategically placed pots, had some colour to set it apart from the flourishing weed patch nearby. Finally, we went for broke and bought a magnificent pot made in terracotta but reinforced with a special ingredient to make it less likely to break. It cost over £100 but the frustration of not being able to develop the land as quickly as we wanted increased our determination to have one large plant at least to show for our efforts by the end of 1991. Into the pot we put an oleander. 'It won't grow,' said Sergio Contini, Ornella's brother confidently, 'You're too high up the side of the hill.' The pot was so huge that once in place we could not move it . . . but the wind did. One day the *Tramontana* blew so hard that over went the giant pot – it's about a metre tall – but the reinforced terracotta mixture lived up to its reputation and survived the fall.

'Hope nobody steals it,' warned the ever-watchful Giulio. So now our prize pot is anchored to the wall of the house, near the entrance to the kitchen, by two metal bands made to measure for us by Domenico Seghini and the oleander every year grows more and more, to provide an enormous display of deep red flowers. We are beginning to get things right.

Pots, no matter how numerous, and how colourful they might be, still left something to be desired in relation to the look of the place. I suppose this was the moment when the gardener, which is buried deep inside all of us, starts to emerge. Maybe the need to command nature is part of the natural instinct of the human race and which, every bit as much as the soul, sets us apart from the rest of animal kind. If you are rich, then you hire the garden designer to do it all for you. So what do you do if you are on a restricted budget? I tried to do the next best thing, talk to a man who knew and might give me the advice for free. Now the only man I knew who might be able to help me was Robert Adams, a landscape architect.

He designed Lord Carrington's garden as well as his own house in Oxfordshire, a mess when he bought it, now a show place, but only for friends, of which we are happy to be included. One weekend as we all sat in the sun behind the house, looking over what seemed to us his well-nigh perfect English garden (it's Robert's judgement there is still a very long way to go before he is really satisfied), I was complaining about the lack of progress in Italy. Truth to tell, I suppose I was trying tactfully to invite Robert and his wife Claire for a free holiday, if he would give me some basic plans to follow.

Robert, who had lived in Italy and in Greece in his earlier years, knew the Mediterranean climate well, but his own business was enjoying a seasonal boom, so he felt he could not leave it even for friends. Of course professionals, like Robert, like doctors and dentists, know instinctively when their brains are being picked, and can quickly but discreetly stop that particular train of thought. He gave me the best advice though: 'What are your neighbours growing? Grow the same as them.' And he showed me a book, now alas out of print, by Georgina Masson on *Italian Gardens*. Try as I could, I never found a copy in any shop, from Foyle's gardening department to the jewel of a secondhand bookshop in Notting Hill. But in the time I had to read her introduction I learned a lot. Ms Masson mentioned the old Roman writers on gardening and agriculture – Cato, Varro, Columella and Pliny. What they said, she suggested, still served in many places in our modern twentieth century.

On winter evenings, when we are in Italy, when the *Tramontana* whistles round the house and the rain beats on the tiles, I read the classic authors, and how right Ms Masson is: the continuity in many farming and growing methods in this part of the world is astonishing. How I wish, for example, that I had read Marcus Cato when I had been negotiating with the Gambacorta sisters over the land: 'When you are thinking of buying a farm keep in mind these points, that you be not over eager in buying nor spare your pains in examining, and that you consider it not sufficient to go over it once. However often you go, a good piece of land will please more at each visit. Notice how the neighbours keep up their places; if the district is good, they should be well kept ... ' And so on went the good Marcus Cato, who farmed two hundred years before Christ in Tusculum. Sometimes the advice given by writers like Varro is of little use, but does give hints of what life could be like for the gentlemen farmers. Varro quotes admiringly Cato's shrewd advice about the number of slaves needed to tend vines and olives, but adds another writer's view on what one slave could achieve, and that the master must allow for such things as illness, bad weather, idleness and laxness.

The slave issue did not concern us because we were working only the equivalent of about three Roman *jugera* – nearly two acres. With Victoria as overseer and me as slave, according to Roman tradition we would be more than enough to work either our vineyard or our olive grove: for our reading had brought us to a choice between wine or oil.

In the end it was Columella, born near Cadiz but who spent his life in Rome in the first century AD, who convinced us in his *De Re Rustica* ('Of Country Matters') that an olive grove was the best bet. As he says, 'The cultivation of any tree is simpler than that of the vine, and the olive tree, the queen of all trees, required least expenditure of all ... It is held in very high esteem because it is maintained by very light cultivation and, when it is not covered with fruit it calls for scarcely any expenditure; also if anything is expended on it, it promptly multiplies its crop of fruit. If it is neglected for several years, it does not deteriorate like the vine ... ' Now, could you have a better recommendation than that? Columella does not stop there but lists ten kinds of olive trees, of which he says the

Licinian produces the best oil. I had forgotten that name, but when we planted our first olives, one of them still had a label tied round a branch – 'Leccino'. Again I felt a sense of continuity with the people who had lived on and worked this land; here was an Englishman, nearly two thousand years later planting a strain of olive favoured by one of the greatest writers on agriculture.

Inevitably, the classic writers could not provide me with the details that I needed for my small plot and so I had to take advice from Giulio who reckoned that fifty olive trees, young ones, would cover enough of the land and produce enough oil at some indeterminate time in the future for our domestic needs. And who knows, one day, if the current olive oil snobbery continues, I might be able to produce a little home-bottled Olio Obday Extra Virgine for the cognoscenti. But let's not mock the olive-oil fanatics, the taste is perfect in this setting and, as Lawrence Durrell put it in his book *Prospero's Cell*: olive oil is a 'taste older than meat, older than wine. A taste as old as cold water.'

At last the property with its olive grove, its pots and its well cut weeds was beginning to look a little more like the home we wanted it to be. It would be five years before we got any oil, five years in which we almost lost the whole lot because of a cold snap one February, the most brutal month in the Umbrian calendar, when suddenly the temperature can nosedive, and the young shoots, misled by the mild days of January when it can be warm enough to go out in shirt-sleeves, are literally nipped in the bud. The Italian word is burned (*bruciate*) and that's how they look with their blackened ends. It was in 1984, I think, when huge swathes of olive groves were burned by the frost; in some places they still have not recovered. The Mancini used to have massive olive trees, they told us, but lost half of them that year. Some of them were at least a hundred years old, planted by their great-great-grandfather when he built the house in which Mr Mancini was born some seventy years ago. Sure enough two years after we planted them, we were hit by frost, losing, so we thought, some ten trees, which had been reduced to nothing more than shrubs. We replaced them, but Marino from Margheriti Brothers told us to plant them in pots, cut off the dead wood and wait.

'They'll come back,' he said. And they have, and been replanted again. So now we have sixty trees, having learned the lesson that the olive tree never really dies. The tree may look dead, but it always grows again. And on some of the most venerable trees, where the trunks, gnarled with age, look like something out of a petrified forest, you will find fresh green shoots springing up from the roots. In time, they will become young sturdy trunks. It's a comforting thought, that whatever happens to our house after we have gone, our sixty olives could and probably will go on growing and producing. I suppose the olives may be the most permanent change we have made to this little plot of land.

After five years we got our first small harvest, about forty pounds of olives, which another neighbour Maria Pazzaglia added to her own huge crop from the grove at the top of the hill, took to the oil-press co-operative and brought us back four litres of oil.

Maria, known near and far by her nickname '*la pupa*' – the kid is for ever on the go – running her house, looking after her husband Mario, and her young son Roberto, who's still at home. She covers countless kilometres a day on her moped, looking after the priest's mother in the morning, feeding her chickens, cooking, cleaning, and keeping up her reputation as the best mushroom finder in the district. She's an extra pair of hands and a source of vegetables, eggs, and recipes whenever we are in

Umbria. And as I say, despite all of this activity, can find time to help us pick our olives.

We have a particular problem gardening at long distance like this. At most, Victoria spends about three months at the house, and I get about six weeks. It means that we are not there always at the right time, so we have to rely on Giulio to make sure that everything that needs doing is done for us. He shoulders the responsibility cheerfully, and divides his time between our land, and about a half a dozen other clients in a similar position. We trust him completely, and he has the keys and the run of the house when we are not there.

Our visits start with a ritual which we all enjoy. We phone Giulio a couple of days before we arrive, and he usually turns up just after breakfast. If the weather's fine we will sit outside under the pergola talking about the land. The conversation goes on for an hour or more; it's rather like a seminar, with Giulio explaining patiently, as if to children, when we need to prune the olives, or the vine, or how to spread manure . . . One day we had the four litres of oil produced from our own olives on the kitchen table and were admiring our handiwork . . . It was one of those startlingly beautiful and warm days that happen in January. The temperature was in the high fifties, and there was not a cloud in the sky.

With the pessimism of a true son of the soil, the good weather did not please Giulio. 'Everything will start to grow,' he told us, 'and then a cold snap next month, and the new growth will die. I don't like this weather.' We need not worry, he said, but should think about those people from Milan who had planted ten thousand olive trees last autumn. 'They've even installed their own oil press . . . I wouldn't like to be in their shoes.' Suddenly my sixty trees seemed less of a problem after all and, when I gave Giulio a bottle of my oil, as a New Year present, I couldn't help saying, 'I hope I can give you more next year, if you are wrong about the frost . . .' Giulio took the bottle and said cryptically: 'At least you had some good oil this year.'

As long-distance gardeners we have one way of keeping in touch with Italian weather. North Kensington has cable television and for a pound a week, we get RAI, the Italian TV channel. In fact, we get more than just the endless game shows and football matches. We also get the Italian equivalent of Ceefax and we can switch to teletext which gives us the weather forecast, with the temperatures recorded the day before and the outlook for the rest of the week. It's a regular ritual at home in London to tune in to Televideo, as it is called, and go through the weather for our region. The nearest city to us is Perugia and so we can see what the maximum and minimum temperatures are day by day. There's fear and worry when the recorded minima go below zero and into the minus figures. Below minus ten the trees could be hit. And there's nothing we can do about it. But we have adopted some of Giulio's pessimism about the weather. By expecting the worst every year, we have much greater joy when we get through February, the cruellest month and into the safer climate of March, when spring really is around the corner.

Even with the olives, the pots and those first trees we planted, the place would never really look right until we created some kind of real garden nearer the house, and separated the garden area from what we call the land, that is, the olive grove. It was in seeking to solve this problem that we incurred the biggest expense outside the house itself, learning, as we did so, some interesting lessons about landscape and architecture.

It took us a year to find the solution and, when we did, it was so obvious it's a wonder we had not thought of it before. The 'simple' answer, of course, was a retaining wall. As so often, though, what started out as a simple little wall, just a foot or so high to mark the boundary, became a massive undertaking ... But let's go back to the beginning. The problem, as I say, was that the land immediately surrounding the house was, so it seemed, incapable of growing anything other than weeds. What's more, it sloped away on one side rather sharply, which meant that the topsoil, as we found to our cost, tended to be washed away when the rains came. The trees managed, just about, to survive the heat and drought of summer, although a prunus, which we had added at the end of one summer, only just kept going until the next summer's drought by being given almost daily watering. Given the lie of the land, the obvious answer was some kind of boundary or retaining wall, which would keep in any topsoil we put down long enough for us to seed it.

Once seeded successfully, we hoped the soil would stay in place, a lawn would emerge and, hey presto, we could have afternoon tea on the lawn like a very proper English couple. The trouble is that you can't just build a wall when you feel like it. You have to submit plans to the town hall in Città della Pieve, and the wall has to be built in keeping with the rest of the house ... so that meant we had to call once more on our friend Sergio Sargentini, the architect and surveyor, who lived over in Tavernelle. A young and rather serious man, Sergio always behaves in the most professional manner, as befits his station in life. He is always dressed in a jacket and a tie. He drives a jeep-like vehicle and always carries a briefcase.

Sergio's plans for the wall turned out to involve much more work than we expected. We had become so used to the sloping terrain on the left-hand side of the house, looking out towards the olives, that we did not realize that to bring the soil up to the level of the right-hand side would involve a wall at least

69

six feet high. On top of which, we would, given the weight of soil behind it, have to have huge foundations, at least four feet down. We also discovered that to level off the soil we would need lorry loads brought up the hill . . . in the end it turned out we needed eighteen lorry loads of soil to fill up the space behind the wall at its deepest point.

For once, though, everything went smoothly: the plans were agreed in double-quick time, Leonardo Pascale, the builder, found a gap in his spring schedule and, within a month, the wall was in place. The brickwork was the same as the house, those rough-hewn chunks of tufa rock and smaller chunks of *cotto*, or baked bricks, all held together with rather uneven cement.

This sort of construction in some ways is a bit of a fraud. It looks old, and does bear some relationship to building styles in the past. But it has now become something of an architectural cliché among us restoring classes. Mind you, it all weathers well and, within a season, the initial rather brash and showy brick and stone has mellowed and the colours softened. But, if I am honest, this style of brickwork is the equivalent of what some antique dealers do in making some wood furniture look 'distressed', as their jargon puts it.

However, the wall, distressed or not, has changed everything. Suddenly the fine old house set in scrubland had been given a base: the wall seemed to make it bigger and more solid. It gave the house roots. The new soil within the wall proved to be as rich as we had hoped and, within a month or two of seeding it, a new lawn began to appear. The weeds, unfortunately, did not disappear but when the grass is cut, it looks fine, much better than the old, dusty, fawn-coloured area that it was before. It took three years to pay off the bank loan but, even when interest rates were at their highest, it turned out to be the best investment of all in the restoration process.

Even our neighbours, who had been anxious while the work was going on, were satisfied and, for a few weeks afterwards, wherever we went, in the local butcher's, the vegetable shop or even to the local restaurant for a quick lunch, everyone congratulated us on the wall.

With the wall in place, everything began to come together. We were still watering by hand every day, pretending as far as we could for the passers-by that it was well water, not from the commune, whose water we were not supposed to use on the garden. It was a two- to three-hour ritual every morning while we were there and even house guests had to do their share of watering. Though I found it terribly boring at first, I began to savour the early morning, when the sun was only just beginning to warm the place, standing there in the fresh morning air, and listening to the birds sing and watching the lizards come out of the cracks in the wall or from under the eaves to settle down to a day's sunbathing and flycatching.

I suppose the best decision we took, at Victoria's insistence, in all the heated debates we had over what to plant and where, was evergreen plants wherever possible. The pine trees, the cypresses, the thulia, and a juniper, that low somewhat squashed-looking fir tree, the laurel and the ivy round the gas tank have all flourished. Even though the weather in December or January can be surprisingly mild, the land itself can look very bleak, with brown branches of the vines now bare. Most of the trees, the robinia and the *pseudoacacia* are just thin branches moving in the wind. The little oaks that grow wild retain their leaves long after the leaves are dead, so you get a brown, burned look on them. The grass is yellow from lack of sun and all the pots are indoors, so there's little colour. But the pines and the Leyland cypress still show dark green against the landscape, while the olives keep their silvery green look all year as well. And the majestic cypress trees may move more in the colder months, as the winds from the north or the south blow across the land, but they still look rich and full of life, standing tall and proud, as they have done for centuries, all over the land. Dark green against a pale winter sun in a largely deserted landscape – winter has its charms every bit as much as summer because of the cypress tree.

They are, I think, my favourite. And I am not alone, every picture of modern Tuscany or Umbria is filled with them, standing tall and straight like sentinels. The tree was just as fascinating to the ancients, who liked to believe it derived from the name of Cyparissus, a handsome young Cretan, whom the god Apollo fancied. The god pursued him but Cyparissus resisted his advances, finally changing himself into a tree.

If there is any frustration about the cypress, it is that it takes its time reaching the height of its growth. And that perfect shape, with all the branches in place and reaching upwards giving it its elongated oval shape, demands a fair amount of judicious pruning: the taller the tree, the harder to prune it. There's a wobbly time for us in early autumn when Victoria, who knows no fear, climbs our longest ladder and cuts off the branches that are sagging out of place.

The construction of the wall created, as I said, a frame into which we could picture more easily where things should go. Impatience took hold and almost before the concrete was dry between the tufa stone, we embarked on another tree-buying spree. Thankfully the pound was strong against the lira when we did it because it gave us a nearly 25 per cent price advantage. We bought ten cypress trees to line the side of the land, creating what would be a very short but very shady walkway between the trees on the one side and the short stretch of wall on the other. Between the trees we planted yet more laurel, which we will leave to grow as high as it likes. In years to come, this should give us a shaded walkway down past the house, along the wall for a few yards and then into the rest of our land, to the fruit trees and the olives.

As always, the frustration is whether we will ever really get the full benefit of the planting, for nature takes its time. Sometimes I envy those whose income allows them to acquire mature trees and derive instant gratification. We've seen century-old olives at the Margheriti Brothers' place and cypress trees that are twice as tall as our house. But then, more often than not, the satisfaction lies in the anticipation of what you might be doing on the land, in the progress that each year brings as the plants survive the winter. We've already achieved an enormous amount but the anticipation of what we might do next, what could go there or there, means that on those winter days when we snatch a week in Italy, by looking to the garden and its future we put down, metaphorically, even deeper roots.

There's an old English proverb that says, in effect, no matter how beautiful the garden, how hard you work, there will always be weeds. In the end, it is by accepting the challenge, and not being too disappointed when nature deals you a harsh blow, that the land and its seasonal rhythms begin to keep you in their thrall. And it is those moments when you've done something that works that are the most satisfying. In my case, it was not so much the plants or trees, as in the construction of the wall. I would never have believed that a retaining wall could bring so much to a piece of uneven and sloping terrain and give the property so much more shape and form. It also allowed us to see more easily what we had achieved. It measured our progress in quite a precise way. Without it, I think we might have been tempted to give up the struggle and our dreams of eventually making our home in Italy would increasingly have turned into nightmares.

I've talked about sweat and tears. What about blood, you ask? I have literally spilt blood creating mine. It's a cautionary tale. We had bought two largish, oblong terracotta pots to put somewhere on the right-hand side of the house, where there is no wall. As always when the weather is fine, we were sitting under the pergola as we had a vigorous conversation about where to site them exactly. Finally, some sort of compromise was reached and I got up to move the very heavy pots, full of soil and flowers but turned and tripped on the edge of the terrace. Over I went, holding on to the pot to save it, and crashed down, smacking my face with great force into the ground and getting cut in the left cheek by a flying piece of terracotta. Blood came spurting out from the artery all over the terrace.

Our neighbours heard the noise, and Victoria's screams at the sight of blood, and came rushing over. The daughter, a chemist, had some first-aid knowledge and managed to get me up and hold the gash together until Victoria drove me and our neighbour to the local hospital in Città della Pieve.

In the casualty room, lying on a table, trying to speak Italian proved too much and I lapsed into the only foreign language I speak fluently, French. Unfazed, the doctor answered in kind and translated for the nurse, who was washing away the still-spurting blood. Three internal stitches, ten external stitches, an X-ray, and I was told to stay in hospital overnight because of what they called my 'cranial trauma'.

Just another accident you say. But not for our friends William and Hilary Keegan, who were coming to lunch that day. They turn up at the house – doors and windows open, no one in sight – only to find on the terrace, a chair knocked over, half-eaten toast, a full cup of cold coffee and blood all over the place. A landlocked *Marie Celeste*. William, like the journalist he is, was on to the story in a flash, checking with the neighbours and at the local café, and arriving at the hospital just as I was being led, still somewhat shaky, to my bed.

I was still wearing a white T-shirt and shorts, both now completely bloodstained. And there was a nurse on either side holding up my eighteen stone frame.

'What on earth happened?' said Bill.

'I was commanding nature,' I said as nonchalantly as I could, 'and nature disobeyed.'

4 In Pursuit of Perugino

SOME MORNINGS THE MIST in the Valley of the Fireflies stays on despite the warming rays of the new day's sun, creating a timeless view of the gentle landscape from the windows of my bedroom. You could be looking out on any century. The mist is wispy white and it clings stubbornly to the tree tops, unwilling to let go. It's on such mornings, were I to follow some old footpath through the oaks and pines, I fancy that I might encounter a rather tubby man in a long black gown, with a red cloth cap on his head. This curious and shapeless piece of headgear holds his rather unkempt longish hair from his eyes. He's broad featured, with a slightly flushed complexion and a thinnish mouth. He doesn't look like a man who would stop to pass the time of day with you, he's obviously off on some sort of business trip. He's riding on a mule, the reins in one hand, the other hand leading another animal with saddlebags behind him. In those bags I might well see some of the tools of his trade. There could be some rolls of kid parchment which, when rubbed with linseed oil, becomes transparent and was used as tracing paper. And if I got a chance to look inside, I might well see some porphyry stone, a small slab and a small block, which was used for grinding colours for paint, or miniver tails for making paint brushes. He'll also have some gold florins hidden away in the saddlebags. Were this chance encounter to take place, he'd be startled to see me, because once on such a journey he was set on and robbed. But he looks like a man not afraid of a fight – he almost went to prison for attempted murder – so I would not want to upset him.

Of course such a meeting can never happen. The man I describe was born in the valley five hundred years ago. His name is Pietro di Cristofero di Vannucci, known to posterity as Il Perugino. He died of the plague, and I think he still haunts the woods and the paths of the country he loved and painted so well and so often.

What I've just described could be the opening sequence from the television documentary I'd like to make one day about Il Perugino's life and times. He lived and painted in a period of great change and danger, a time of superstition, plague and famine, a time of invasion when even Florence was occupied by foreigners. But it was also a time of great intellectual achievement, ideas being spread by the new invention of the printing press. A time when mankind was asking questions about the meaning of life that had not been asked since the days of Plato or Socrates. It was a world which, in the memorable phrase of the American historian William Manchester, was 'lit by fire'. Through all of this, this short stocky man went about his chosen profession with dedication, all the while turning out for his many patrons paintings and frescos which all called 'sweet' and in all of which can be glimpsed the presence of Lake Trasimeno in the background of a saucer-shaped landscape, where the young acacia trees, with their springtime tracery of small leaves, stand in serried ranks on the gentle slopes that rise from the water's edge.

It must have been fate that led me from my house to this figure from the past who, over the years, has unlocked the door through which I could travel back in time and start to appreciate so much of the history of Umbria and its place in the Renaissance. Pietro, the painter from my small village, has become the focus for most of my research. Initially it was just diversion, something to underpin my book-buying, allowing me to look up my man in the index. The process was neither planned nor structured in any way. I didn't work out any sort of study programme. Again that Lawrence Durrell quote comes back to mind: 'Journeys, like artists, are born and not made. A thousand differing circumstances contribute to them, few of them willed . . .' Well, this exactly describes the early days of my quest for Perugino, a quest that has led me back as far as the Romans and the Greeks, to an increasingly detailed study of the popes and princes in Italy between 1400 and 1550, and has taken me to places I would never have thought of visiting, to churches and museums I would have walked past. Perugino now sneaks up on me unexpectedly. For example, when I was having the water from my new well analysed in the nearby village of Panicale, while I waited for the results I popped into the church nearby, largely to escape the sun's heat on my bald head. And what do I see, but Perugino's *Martyrdom of San Sebastiano*.

At first, Perugino-spotting was an idle pastime. What hooked me, irrevocably, was a line I came across in an old book, published privately in the 1920s, by a local priest in Città della Pieve who, like me, had become obsessed with

Perugino. Don Canuti collected everything he could about the painter. He traced every known document, every reference and almost every picture. Whenever any scholar today talks of Perugino, they always quote either Giorgio Vasari, who was born in the sixteenth century a few years after Perugino's death and didn't really like the man, or Canuti, who worked in the early years of this century and who hero-worshipped him.

Everyone reads Vasari, an artist in his own right, an architect, but most of all the author of the *Lives of the Artists*, the first attempt to draw up standards of judgement on art and artists. But Vasari had his enthusiasms and his pet theories, which can trap the unwary amateur like me, if you read him first without any prior knowledge at all. Luckily George Bull, a former colleague of mine from my days in print journalism, was Vasari's translator for the Penguin edition, and he warned me. Fortunately, I soon discovered the other great source – how, I'll explain later – Don Canuti, the parish priest. It was Canuti who speculated as to whether Pietro Vannucci, one of three sons born to a local farmer, first saw the light of day within the walls of the small town, or down in, you've guessed it, the Valley of the Fireflies, where the Vannucci family had some land, with olives and lines of vines between the trees, just as our neighbours do today a little farther up our hill.

I admit that this kind of claim is of the 'Queen Elizabeth the First once slept here' variety. Perhaps I should say, since this is Italy, 'Garibaldi once stayed here'. It's obviously a claim easily made and, given the circumstances of his birth, impossible to either prove or disprove. As for so many at the time born outside the big cities, there is no birth certificate. So we don't know exactly where he was born, or on what day of what month of what year. The best guess is between 1445 and 1450. But once I had discovered the possible 'fact' that my valley could have been his birthplace, I became addicted, and like any addict, went to almost any lengths to get a 'fix'. After nearly half a decade on the Perugino trail, I am still hooked.

In many ways it's become a detective story, trying to find new clues to one of the most prolific yet shadowy figures of the period. The writer Michael Dibdin's fictional Italian detective, Aurelio Zen, would jump at the chance, because here is a quarry worthy of his insight into human nature. What's more, Perugino had a police record. He was always the successful outsider: written off by some, highly valued by others, Perugino is always mentioned in the textbooks and the histories by the art world's experts yet somehow, literally as well as figuratively, he remains in the margin. What a pity Don Canuti is no longer alive – with today's technology who knows what he might have been able to unearth. I am convinced that somewhere, either in Perugia where the artist spent his last years, or in Florence where he began his glittering career, or maybe in the huge archives of the Vatican where he was the first artist to lead a team to paint the Sistine Chapel, there's a scrap of paper or two that will provide more clues to this man. I am convinced there's a treasure trove waiting to be dug from the archives which will put him back where he used to be, the equal of his famous contemporaries, Leonardo da Vinci and Michelangelo.

If I ever make my film, I want someone like Derek Jacobi to play the part of Don Canuti, who would be the storyteller. I'd sit him on an ornate chair in the middle of the Collegio del Cambio, the bankers' hall in Perugia. Here you can see Pietro's master work painted with the help of the young Raphael. The irony for me is how a humble parish priest could become hooked on Perugino, because Pietro hated the Church. Yet the Church was Perugino's main patron. He was, says Vasari, an atheist and a blasphemer, a common trait, I'm told among people from Perugia, who have a long history of fighting against the popes in Rome. And yet it was a priest who worked so hard, not to save his soul, but his reputation. Don Canuti, alias Derek Jacobi, would meet some interesting people in the film because Perugino was also an almost exact contemporary of Leonardo da Vinci and Botticelli who were, with him, students and workers in the workshop of the sculptor Verrocchio in Florence in the 1470s.

Although he was born in or near Città della Pieve, he is known to all by his nickname, Il Perugino, from the city of Perugia, which ruled his tiny birthplace. Can you imagine in a world like his that Il Pievese would have had the same ring to it? It's a great trivial pursuit question, though: can you give Il Perugino's real name and where he was born? It's an odd fact that, but many of the great painters and sculptors of the period were known by such nicknames. Perugino used it himself because, like so many of his contemporaries, he knew that a distinctive nickname – perhaps we'd call it a 'brand name' – meant he could be immediately recognized and placed.

Some day there ought to be a full-length academic study of these sobriquets, because they seem to say so much about the people who 'traded' under them. They also explain their place in the system, at the start of a process by which artists became known as individuals. Mind you, not all such nicknames were as straightforward as Pietro's. Botticelli means the little beer barrel, while Verrocchio – 'true eye' – was not applied to the artist himself because of his own undeniable talent, but because he was taught by an ecclesiastic of that name.

Some of the other painters of around Perugino's time sound equally uninspired when rendered into English. Uccello, for example, means 'birdman'. Antonio del Pollaiuolo was so called because his father was a poultry keeper and the great Tintoretto because his father was a dyer by trade, so the artist became the 'little dyer'. Two of Perugino's pupils and coworkers were dubbed 'Pintoricchio', which means literally 'rich colour' and 'L'ingegno', which means 'brains'. Some names tell you something about an individual. Take Giorgione, for example, a known *bon viveur* and lover of wine, woman and song, the name, literally translated is 'Big George'. Another artist, Antonio Rossellino, means 'little redhead'. Many artists, like Perugino, were named after the place whence they came: Parmigianino, from Parma; Veronese from Verona; Correggio from Correggio and Jacopo Bassano from, yes you've guessed, Bassano. What a wonderful cast of characters any documentary would have, for Pietro knew and worked with many of these men. And competed successfully with them too for some of the bigger commissions, making him one of the wealthiest painters of his day. Vasari tends to dismiss him as being obsessed with money, and something of a miser. But then Vasari, no mean collector of commissions himself, had strong views as to how a painter should behave: he should be devoted to his work, seeking only to improve himself and his art. Vasari put Pietro's obsession with money down to the fact that he was born in poverty. But then Vasari was a bit of a snob, which is why I think I see him played by Brian Sewell, the art critic. I've never met Mr Sewell but he haunts a second-hand bookshop in Notting Hill that has provided me with many a happy find. Mr Sewell has just the sort of accent that I fancy Vasari adopted when he talked about the painters of his day. Vasari loosely translated means 'potter'.

Vasari has to be respected but he did not always get things right. Perugino was not born in poverty. According to Don Canuti, the Vannucci family owned land, paid taxes and were on the town council. So Pietro cannot have been as poor as Vasari makes out. But then wealth, in the context of a tiny place like Città della Pieve, is relative and Pietro had to leave to seek his fortune.

When he arrived in Florence, we don't know. But since he would start young, it must have been around 1460. All we do know is that in the 1470s he suddenly appears in the artists' guild in Florence, the Company of St Luke. He is listed as 'Pietro di Cristofano da Perugia'. From then on, notes Canuti, he was known to all and sundry as Il Perugino. Obviously in those early years Perugino joined a workshop, some say it was Verrocchio's, the favourite artist of the ruling family in Florence, the Medici. But no one is really sure. Vasari says he worked hard at his painting, only stopping to sleep a little and eat less, he was so poor. But we can imagine life as an apprentice, because that is what, in effect, these young, would-be artists were. You get some idea from *The Craftsman's Handbook (re Libro dell'Arte)* by Cennino di Drea Cennini, which first appeared in manuscript form in 1437, just before widespread printing was to give it such extensive circulation in the later years of the century, when Perugino was at his peak. Cennini is full of advice on how to enter the trade: 'You . . . who are . . . about to enter the profession, begin by decking yourselves with this attire: enthusiasm, reverence, obedience and constancy. And begin to submit yourself to the direction of a master for instruction as early as you can; and do not leave the master until you have to.'

A steady hand is what is needed, says Cennini, and the advice he gives here was ignored by Perugino and most artists: 'Your life should always be arranged just as if you were studying theology, or philosophy or other theories, that is to say eating and drinking moderately at least twice a day . . . wholesome dishes and light wines.' Don't lift heavy stones, or work with huge crowbars, he says, as this will tire your hand, and he goes on: 'There is another cause which if you indulge in it, can make your hand so unsteady that it will waver more and flutter far more, than leaves do in the wind and this is

83

indulging too much in the company of women.' Now that's advice I'm sure Pietro ignored, while had Raphael listened to it, he might well have lived longer rather than, as some claim, shortening his life by over-indulgence with the groupies who surrounded him.

The handbook, though, is more than just a moral tract, it is a practical guide to the work of the artist, from making colours, mixing paints, making plaster casts from the dead and the living, working in fresco, metal, stone, everything that the artist or artisan of the time might need. I can't resist giving his advice (I've shortened it somewhat) on making miniver brushes: 'Miniver tails should be cooked and not raw . . . first pull out the tip of it, because these are the long hairs . . . take the straightest and firmest hairs from the middle of the tail . . . wash them in clear water . . . put them into bunches and trim with a small pair of scissors . . . then make your brushes in the size you want. Some will fit in a vulture's quill, some to fit in a goose's quill.' I wonder how many hours a young apprentice spent making these brushes, or even the tougher variety from hog's hair – the white hog is better than the black hog, says Cennini, and make sure they are domestic animals. The final touch is to bind these hairs tight with a small thread or waxed silk. Perugino would have learned all this during his years in Verrocchio's workshop. Cennini was passing on the skills developed a century or more before by Giotto and, in turn, Perugino no doubt passed them on to Raphael.

Perugino's natural talent and ability to work hard soon began to establish him in Florence, which was then the centre for artists. Rather like the song says, 'if you could make it there, you could make it anywhere.' It was only towards the end of the fifteenth century, when he was in his fifties, that Perugia began to give him work and he started to buy property in his hometown of Città della Pieve for his old age and his growing family.

In Città della Pieve, these days, it's impossible to escape the little red-brick walled town's most famous son. They've named a street after him, the Via Vannucci and there are two wall plaques, one in the Via Vannucci and the other in the main square, claiming that Pietro lived there or was born there. In the *duomo*, once a cathedral, but now downgraded because they no longer appoint bishops to Città della Pieve, you are immediately told that there is a copy of the painter's most famous self portrait, in which he calls himself *Pictor Castris Plebis*. I wonder how often Don Canuti looked upon this picture: there's that red work cap to keep the paint off his hair, those flushed cheeks and the rather thin, even cruel, lips, and that proud boast about being a master painter. Nowadays you can buy that likeness on a postcard; I have one in a small, simple frame near my computer as I write. But Don Canuti would have seen the pictures by the master. He would not have far to travel for that. Don Canuti in his hat and long black soutane, looking not a little like a figure from the Renaissance himself, had but to walk a few hundred metres down the narrow street from the *duomo* to see Perugino's *Visitation of the Magi* which has just been restored in a small oratory in the Via Vannucci. It was here that the restorers found tucked in behind some brickwork a letter from Perugino to one of his clients. We do not know whether he could read or write – it might have been written for him – but the language is straight and direct and the phonetic spelling lets you almost hear his accent, broad Umbrian, no doubt, which would have made him something of an outsider in sophisticated Florence.

Like all obsessives, I used to talk about Pietro to everyone who would listen. It's also a very journalistic habit. Like fishing, if you cast your net wide enough, you never know what you might land. That's how I discovered the old priest Don Canuti and his monumental labour of love. I asked Giancarlo Caponeri, who seems to know everyone, whom I could talk to in Città della Pieve who might let me see some of the Perugino papers. He said the man to see was the cultural officer, Valerio Bitarello.

I phoned him and he accepted at once my invitation to meet. Signor Bitarello is a busy man, endlessly arranging exhibitions in the fourteenth-century Palazzo della Corgna, the town hall, one of a number of buildings that Perugino would recognize today. In his time he has arranged not only for painters to show their art, but workers in wrought iron, master carpenters, as well as musicians and sculptors. It is one of the wonders of these small towns (Città della Pieve has around 5,000 inhabitants), that they get such facilities. But Bitarello does more . . . he's involved in the annual *palio* where many of the townspeople dress in fifteenth-century costume and parade through the narrow streets, looking for all the world like a crowd from a Perugino painting. Given all this hard work and the enthusiasm with which this short, bearded and intense man does everything, he was not at all put out when an Englishman rings him up out of the blue and says he wants to talk about Perugino.

We duly met in a local bar and over espresso he spoke long and fluently about Città della Pieve's main claim to world fame. Much of what he said passed over my head, it was more a performance than a conversation. But he did offer me one marvellous lead. In the library in Città della Pieve was a copy of the standard work on Pietro's life, written in the 1920s by the local priest Don Fiorello Canuti. He had had it printed privately, five hundred copies, and had gone to his grave a happy man, his life's work completed. Valerio would make arrangements for me to consult the copies that were in the library in the Palazzo della Corgna.

The next day I drove up into the town and went into the library. Signor Bitarello had kept his word. The two volumes were waiting for me. They are a treasure trove, these books, so lovingly compiled by the old priest who had made it his life's work in between baptizing, marrying and burying generations of Pievese. There was a problem though: while I could follow the modern Italian, though the priest had a somewhat baroque style it must be said, I was stumped when I tried to read the actual source documents copied in their original Tuscan or, more often than not, the Latin. At that time, printing was only just beginning to make its presence felt in the world of letters and as yet there was no standard spelling for many words. Most of these documents were written by hand, so the spellings varied as to how the writer heard the words ... even Vannucci's name might have been written slightly differently. As we've seen when he was inscribed in the Company of St Luke, he was called di Cristofano, not di Cristofero; perhaps he had a slight cold that day as he dictated his name, so the 'er' became an 'an'.

Apart from the language, the problem was compounded by the fact that Don Canuti was more of a researcher than a writer, so he gave you lists and dates. What you get are the bare bones of a life; rarely do you glimpse the man of the flesh. Yet Canuti was intrigued by him and in his book you hear about Pietro getting involved in a drunken brawl, being accused of attempted murder and there's a reference to a homosexual relationship with a young apprentice (in other words, sex and violence, the very necessary ingredients for a modern TV documentary). In this Perugino was not alone – many of the great artists were actively homosexual, or bisexual, and you can find many texts condemning the sin of sodomy in Florence.

Canuti's lists also show you what a hugely peripatetic life the painter led, as he trekked across the countryside to fulfil his commissions and, remember, most of his travelling was by mule, or on horseback. So back and forth he went, from Florence to Perugia, to Città della Pieve, to Rome, to Florence, carrying his paints and brushes with him, and his gold.

These lists were what gave me the germ of the idea to try to write my version of Perugino's life, a reconstructed life, following the artist's progress from country bumpkin with talent, to rich and respected artist, the most sought-after of his day, to the final years when, no longer quite in the mainstream, he went on painting his madonnas for lesser patrons, like yesterday's pop singer doing the round of the supper clubs in middle America, still earning a crust, still meeting his fans, but looking enviously at the new kids on the block. In Pietro's case, these were Raphael his pupil, who so quickly outshone him, and Michelangelo, who once called him a buffoon. Pietro even sued Michelangelo for the insult but he lost his case.

The problem with my 'obsession', was that the need to earn my living kept intervening and, no sooner had I got down to some serious reading about Perugino, than I was thundering down the *autostrada del sole* to Fiumicino for a flight home and four a.m. starts on the *Today* programme. Once though, after a lot of work on Pietro, I found myself back in the studio in London interviewing the chancellor of the exchequer, Kenneth Clarke and, for a moment or two, in the subdued light of the studio, Mr Clarke looked rather like Pietro . . . the same ever so slightly unkempt look, the chubby cheeks and the brazen eye that looks straight at you and dares you to try it on. Are they by any chance related, I wonder?

So far I've made no grand discoveries. I'm slowly coming to the conclusion though that Pietro's life does need properly investigating, covering as he does the key period of the Renaissance, and knowing, as he did, all the key artistic players. The problem is that modern critics tend to dismiss him as being repetitive, the same stock poses, the eyes turned upward to heaven, the hands held together in prayer. The faces, especially of his madonnas, all look the same. It's said they are of his young wife Clara whom he married in the 1490s. She must have been a beauty.

Signor Bitarello dismisses those critics who say that Pietro was repetitive: 'Are pop stars repetitive when they sing their latest hit over and over again? Was Andy Warhol repetitive when he made prints of a Campbell's soup can? People wanted to own the Perugino that they had seen on someone else's wall, and they were prepared to pay top money to get it. Given the time in which he lived, do you blame him for giving the public what they wanted?'

It's a strong argument, especially when one takes into account the power of the patron and the reasons for patronage. In almost all cases, the idea of a public display of power, rather than wealth, meant that the artist was also a propagandist. Even Michelangelo had to fight hard to get popes to see things his way. The popes always felt that since they were paying the painter, they could tell them what to draw. Indeed the worst painting that Perugino did, and the one which has the best history, is the picture he painted for Isabella d'Este from Mantua. Isabella would be a marvellous character for my film. She was rich, powerful and determined to be the best known patron of the arts. Were she still on the stage, I would ask Glenda Jackson, now a Labour member of Parliament, to take the role of Isabella. She would be perfect in the part of the Renaissance blue-stocking. Isabella wrote to everyone who was anyone at the time to commission them. Leonardo managed to elude her grasp but others, like Mantegna, were not able to resist. From Perugino, Isabella d'Este wanted a small picture, smaller in size than most of Pietro's work. And she chose the subject herself, a subject that I think Perugino would have found difficult to imagine. Isabella wanted the struggle between vice and virtue . . . not a struggle that the painter himself would have undergone often. But Isabella went even further. She told him what figures she wanted and where, what the size would be, when she wanted it delivered and how she wanted it painted. The money was good, so Pietro reluctantly accepted the commission, taking more than five years to complete it. He was never happy with it, resisting all the way. We have some of the letters they exchanged, and the comments of her agents, whom she sent after Pietro to chivvy him along.

'Where were you when my agent called?' she pleaded more than once, 'when will I have my picture . . .'

Everyone agreed with her that he was one of the greatest painters of the time. Whether it was because she believed that she had the better taste or not, however, she did not commission a typical Perugino. Although contemporaries used the word 'sweet' to describe his style, somehow the English word does not quite convey what the original Italian *dolce* means in this context. Perhaps the translation should be 'soft' or even 'gentle', illustrated best perhaps in the face of a Perugino Madonna, where there is a marvellous sense of innocence, of purity of feature. If there is one sphere where Pietro was unsurpassed, it was in rendering the human face. Add to that those distant saucer-shaped landscapes with lake and trees stretching to infinity, and the use of the paint, the gradations of colour, and you understand why he was in such demand, producing a view of the world that contrasted with the nastiness of much contemporary life. Maybe that was his appeal; while most people worried about survival, while the powerful clashed and struggled, while famine and plague still persisted,

Perugino would give you a landscape where the world was always in springtime, with delicately rendered young trees, which allowed you to enjoy the view, through their thin branches and budding leaves, of a lake so pale and calm and with skies that went from almost white at the water's edge to the deepest blue at the very top of the picture.

Yet the man, says Vasari in his bitchy biography, could be a foul-mouthed, blasphemous, money-mad thug. Was he so different from many of his patrons, the Borgias and the popes, who made money or sex their god? Perugino lived at a time when the Church's corruption was known by most, and actively opposed by many. He would have been in Florence often during the 1490s, the time of Savonarola, the monk burnt at the stake for his attacks on the vice and corruption in Rome. It was an age of great learning but of great cynicism as well. Why should Perugino be any different? For those who have studied his paintings, it's commonly accepted that in his later years his assistants did most of the work, while he did the marketing.

Is this really the sort of character about whom one can build the biography of his age, so talented and yet so deeply flawed? Why not? The odd thing about the man is that he appeals differently to different ages. In the eighteenth century, Oliver Goldsmith's advice was 'always praise a Perugino' and, in the last century, the Pre-Raphaelites admired him. In this century, he's seen as arid and repetitive. Will it change again after the year 2023, which would be the five hundredth anniversary of his death? But, as our world changes before our eyes, maybe Perugino's hard-won fortune in an age where nothing could be taken for granted will appeal again. As Bernard Berenson, the great American art historian wrote: 'He had a feeling for beauty in women, charm in young men and dignity in the old, seldom surpassed before or since.'

So I pressed ahead with my research. Since I could not talk to Don Canuti, I did the next best thing, and got in touch with Professor Pietro Scarpellini, at Perugia University, who produced the definitive work on all of Pietro's pictures and frescos. We arranged to meet outside the university's arts department and tried to describe ourselves to each other: we both claimed to be middle-aged, with white hair, and a little on the portly side. From his description of himself, I knew I'd like him.

In fact I recognized him at once; there is something about Italian professors that marks them out from the crowd – less chic, slightly more crumpled, but always with books and bundles of newspapers under the arm and the hair just a little on the wild side. Professor Scarpellini took me to a café in front of the Collegio del Cambio in the pedestrian precinct that Perugia's city fathers have ordained for their fine city. It's called the Corso Vannucci, what else, and in the national gallery of Umbria, which is almost next door to the Collegio del Cambio, there's a marvellous collection of Perugino's art as well as work by his contemporary Umbrian artists and collaborators like Pinturicchio.

At first it was a disappointing encounter. The professor could not tell me much more than I already knew . . . had I read Canuti, had I seen his book? It was 'yes' to both questions. Had I seen the Cambio? I told him my interest in the artist came after they had started a massive restoration programme.

Without a moment's pause he said, 'Come with me' and off Victoria and I trooped to the Cambio. A knock at the door, a whispered conversation and we were inside, with all the lights on, and no one else in sight. The professor took us up some of the ladders and, for the next hour, treated us to what can only be described as the ultimate seminar on Perugino and his working methods.

The Cambio is quite a shock to the senses when you see it for the first time, if you are expecting a 'typical' Perugino. The walls and the ceilings are covered with pictures depicting classical scenes. The work had been commissioned by a leading humanist in Perugia, Francesco Maturanzio. There are characters such as Prudence and Justice, and prophets like Isaiah, Moses, Daniel, there are sibyls, and figures like Mercury, drawn in winged chariots by fantastic creatures. But, like all humanists, Maturanzio could not just have life before Christ as his inspiration, so there was a Nativity as well as God himself. For Perugino it must have been quite a challenge, for he was painting images that were nowhere to be seen in his usual commissions. The work took many years, and you can see the painstaking attention to detail.

'You see those tiny holes there,' said Professor Scarpellini as we got so close to the wall that our noses were almost touching, 'those are where he held the tracing paper in place. That dust could be the dust of the period.' Then, at another point, he'd lean forward, as enthusiastic as any good teacher and say, 'See that brush stroke, you can see how he applied the paint, you can see the direction.' I wondered quietly and to myself, whether he had used a brush made of miniver tail hairs held in a goose quill, just as Cennini had instructed.

'You can imagine him here can't you?' Professor Scarpellini went on, 'in his red hat, in a dusty, sweaty atmosphere, carefully working away at the pictures, but keeping one eye on young Raphael, his most famous pupil, who would no doubt be colouring or tracing another scene for the master to finish . . .'

What makes the Cambio achievement even more remarkable was that all of this artistic endeavour was going on while what is claimed to be Italy's most violent city was going through another of its monumental internecine struggles for power between the Oddi and the Baglioni families, the main rivals for power in Perugia. But the massacre this time is still remembered as 'the great betrayal' because it happened during the prolonged wedding celebrations of a young Baglioni, called Astorre, to Lavinia, a member of the powerful Roman clan, the Colunna. Conspirators worked on the young men of the family, claiming that cousins had seduced sisters. Dozens were killed every day in the street fighting between the clans; their bodies, ripped by daggers or hacked by swords, had been left where they fell oozing blood on the paving stones of the main square. Finally, Gianpaolo Baglioni, who was to rule for a dozen years until betrayed by a pope, extracted a massive revenge. More than a hundred conspirators were executed, and their heads stuck on spikes around the Prior's Palace. The leaders were painted in fresco but upside down. And he ordered the cathedral to be washed down with wine and reconsecrated. Yet, such was the way of the world, that in a building almost next door to the Prior's Palace, a master painter on top of his form and his star pupil Raphael were creating scenes from the classical world meant to inspire all who saw them to a more humanist view of life.

Perugino was very proud of Collegio del Cambio ... and he has every right to be. He painted, as if it were a picture hanging on the wall, his own portrait in a gilded frame. A copy of it is in Don Canuti's church in Città della Pieve. Perhaps he already sensed that as the fifteenth century gave way to the sixteenth he would soon be past his best. Perugino was the archetypal self-made man, which is why he felt able, without any trace of embarrassment, to put underneath his self-portrait in the Cambio this proud boast written in Latin:

'Even were the art of painting to have become lost, here, by the distinguished Pietro of Perugia was it restored. Had it nowhere been devised at this level, he gave it to us. In the year of our saviour 1500.'

Hubris. Soon after fashion changed in Florence, and Perugino was no longer seen by the Florentines as having much to offer. Proud though he was, I have to say that in my book he never really fell that far. In his fifties, he still got commissions from smaller towns and villages, still anxious to have their very own Perugino. Mostly he worked in Umbria, the local boy made good. Another professor wrote in his history of the Renaissance that Michelangelo and Raphael arrived at the threshold to high mannerism. Perugino, says Professor Frederick Hartt, was temperamentally unable to cross it and so remains a man of the late fourteenth century, not of the fifteenth.

Barely twenty years later, at what was a ripe old age in that period, of seventy plus, Perugino would die with a brush still in his hand, working on another madonna, not in some gilded place like the Cambio but in a humble country chapel midway between Città della Pieve and Perugia itself. I put off going there for as long as I could, I wanted to see more of Perugino in his glory before I contemplated him at his end.

You can see Peruginos in almost every west European country, that dreadful picture he painted for Isabella d'Este is in the Louvre, but he's in the National Gallery in London, in Washington and New York, in Vienna. Almost every major gallery has a Perugino of sorts ... in all there are some three hundred attributed wholly or partially to him or his workshops.

And there are many of them scattered in the small country churches in and around his birthplace. I've mentioned the *Martyrdom of San Sebastiano* in Panicale. It was later that I discovered that for a long time the picture was covered with a cloth because it was thought the naked body of the martyr would inflame the senses of the women of the parish. There are Peruginos, but no nudes, in three churches in his home town of Città della Pieve. You can find him in Siena, where it's said his very first teacher, name unknown, came from.

For me, though, the place to feel the man's presence is where, in his seventies, he painted his last fresco, working alone in the winter of 1523 in a private chapel, in a place called Fontignano midway along the road between Città della Pieve and Perugia. It was a road he must have travelled hundreds of times and I suppose to die half-way along it, between the place where he was born, and the city whose name he adopted as his own, in a church in whose God he did not believe, was a summary of his whole life. The subject was the *Baptism of Christ*. According to Don Canuti, he had the plague, and he died alone; when his body was discovered by some local people, they threw the plague-ridden remains into a ditch and covered them up. Can you blame them, what with the plague then ravaging the countryside and the cities? Better a live peasant than a dead art lover.

Don Canuti goes on to tell how later there was a hunt for the remains of the famous painter: a skeleton was found, which seemed to match Pietro's known height, around five feet, and it was buried with all due pomp and ceremony. Later, in this little out of the way chapel, a grandiose plaque was put on the wall lauding Pietro and his life. And there's a bronze medallion shewing Pietro, the likeness taken from his self-portrait but here in relief which gives it added interest. It is sad that this small place is locked and the key is kept nearby in a local café and, unless you know that, you can't gain entrance. On the other hand, if you are in the know, then at least you can go in by yourself and not be disturbed. Even on the hottest day, the place is as cold as the grave. It's easy to imagine how glacial it must have been in 1523, in the coldest month of the Umbrian year, February, when a seventy-year-old man, riddled with the plague, his fingers freezing as he tries to apply the paint, is, as Canuti gently puts it, 'surprised by death'. That would obviously make a telling end to my documentary, filmed in the place where it happened, even though the actual picture has long been in the National Gallery in London. There's even the local church bell which tolled while I was there, adding a further dimension to the pictures.

There's one other sequence for the film which I would prefer to leave you with, not sad thoughts of death, but of art in action. The idea came from a chance conversation with some friends of ours: they had a house at the time near Orvieto, whose cathedral had once commissioned Perugino to do some work but could not agree a price. (In the end, it was Luca Signorelli, a close friend of Pietro's, who did the work, to his everlasting fame.) Tosi d'Amato is an art dealer, and we were talking about the possibility of a Perugino ever coming on to the market.

'The only way you'll get anything like a Perugino is to ask my friend Eric Hebborn to paint you one.'

That was how the idea came to have Hebborn, if he would, paint me a Perugino in fresco so that the film could be punctuated by sequences of his progress. This way one could see the artist at work, explain more about the method of painting in fresco and, at the same time, create a picture from the first drawings on paper to the finished piece. When Hebborn's book on his success in fooling the art world was published, we were invited to the launch, thanks to Tosi d'Amato. Hebborn perpetrated his simple deception by using paper and paints from the age, or reproduced in the traditional manner, so as not to be immediately apparent as a modern piece of work. Obviously Hebborn was a close student of Cennini's little handbook for artists, as he mixed the colours and drew the lines so well. Posing as an art dealer, he included the results with other genuine pictures when he showed his portfolio to the world's leading galleries and auction houses. More often than not it was the 'expert' who exclaimed, on coming across a 'Hebborn':

'But that's a drawing by Raphael.'

'Is it really?' Eric would reply, accepting with surprise that the picture he had included in his portfolio was given such an attribution. Yet the pictures were usually of subjects that the artist in question had never actually drawn himself. Eric chose the subject matter, but executed it in the manner of the chosen artist. So Eric said, they were not forgeries, since he was not copying an existing picture or print. Eric, therefore, would be the perfect choice for the film, executing as he would, in such an 'authentic' manner the craft of one of the great fresco painters of the fifteenth century. In close up, Eric's hands would star as the hands of Pietro at work. In a wide shot, dressed in the costume of the era, we would see a real artist at work.

It was Victoria who asked him if he would consider the assignment, should we find a backer for the film. A local Perugia savings bank, the Casa di Risparmio, had financed the restoration of the Cambio so, at the time I thought maybe I could approach them while they were still in a Perugino frame of mind.

'As long as the cheque does not bounce,' was Eric's reply.

But where could we paint such a fresco, which would in itself be a work of art? We still had one room to restore in the house in the Valley of the Fireflies. Why not there? It would enhance the room and, in a way, would bring Perugino back to life in his home village. I would have a room with a marvellous fresco and, who knows in years to come, long after I too have been 'surprised by death', some art critic will happen upon the house and, wonder of wonders behold, what he or she believes to be a genuine Perugino. Maybe this was even the house where he was born ... All the textbooks would have to be revised. And this fresco would be just a little bit better than most, and in such amazing condition that the artist's reputation would suddenly be looked at again and his true genius recognized by a new generation ... All because of a skilfully executed fresco on the wall of a farmhouse in Umbria. Eric and I, and no doubt Don Canuti, will look down and smile at the ways of the world, and how easy it is to fool some of the people a lot of the time. And if we are really lucky maybe Pietro too will be there to tell Eric how he would have done it and, no doubt, how much he would have asked for as his fee ...

5 Luigi Venturini's Well

THE MOST FRUSTRATING and, in some ways, most worrying aspect of developing the house in Umbria was when we decided to sink a well. Everyone asked when we would have one, everyone said that a house without a well was no better than a house without a roof. Land with water on it meant wealth indeed. 'It's worth more than money,' said Giulio Cerboni. But as in all things you need to speculate to accumulate and in the end we acquired not only some water but more insight into what makes Italy in general, and Umbria in particular, tick.

It was when we were in the last stage of the project that the frustrations grew fastest, so let me start near the end, before I go back to the beginning. Imagine a hot day in July. The birds are singing, the earth slowly baking, and the plants turning the palest shade of brown in the drought which has lasted two months. The well was due to be started and we had a putative date. That day came and went. Then we moved into what chess players call 'the end game'.

First, a man turned up unannounced and asked questions. He seemed to be looking for someone but his questions were largely incomprehensible; they were expressed in a thick regional accent and with a determination on his part not to speak the flatter, slower Italian that most locals adopt when they quickly realize you are not from hereabouts. His look, 'more of a leer' thought Victoria, had the effect of scaring Victoria and her friend Kate Goslet, a house guest, because they thought he was up to no good. Indeed Kate, a psychotherapist, fresh out from England, thought he must be the local rapist come to check out the place before he carried out his attacks. As a defence, she suggested that Victoria wash a pair of my underpants and a pair of cotton trousers and hang them out on the clothes line, to suggest that there was a man in the house who would make sure he did not get his evil way. Not the most politically correct course of action, I remarked, when I heard the story but flattered that in the 1990s the male presence should still count for something.

The threatening stranger turned out not to be a rapist but the man who dug the well, one Renato Bracchi from Chiusi. Four days after his visit, a small blue and white lorry turned up and parked in among the olives. On the side of the door on the driver's side, a faded piece of paper, only just adhering to the metal, gave his name and his business – the drilling and boring of artesian wells. The lorry had seen better days: it was a small miracle, no doubt thanks to Saint Francis of nearby Assisi, that it had made it up the hill and on to our land. But at least it promised some action because on the back was a rusting, and in parts oily, black contraption that passed for a gantry crane with which the well would be dug.

The vehicle was parked there for four days and no one came

near it. Then Renato came back and looked over the spot where we wanted the well dug. Renato shook his head in a knowing fashion, scratched his chin, smiled an ingratiating smile and began to give us the benefit of his many years in the well business.

Like all Italians Renato had his own firmly held opinions about what we should do. For starters he suggested that we had not got the would-be well in the right place. He said putting a well down alongside the olive grove was wrong and we would not get much water. Renato reckoned, we should put it nearer the house where, he assured Victoria, there was water aplenty. One felt a whiff of self-interest here, I must say, because where Renato wanted to put the well was in a better location, I had to admit, but it was much deeper. He reckoned about a hundred metres, as opposed to the spot we had fixed on, where the water was said to be about fifty metres down. At an estimated £60 pounds a metre, another fifty metres made the whole proposition almost double the original estimate. And even then we could not be sure until we struck water.

It was all based on what the local water diviner, Luigi Venturini, had told us when his elm twigs twitched violently a year before. Of Luigi more later, but then, as I say, all Italians have an opinion about things. What's more, their opinion is always at variance with one's own. It may be just a way of getting a conversation going; it may be because a good debate makes life worth living; it may be a kind of *bella figura* where appearances count for more than anything else, or it may just be because Italians find it difficult to stay silent when they meet people. For example, Giovanni, our Roman friend who lives on the next hill, told us that there was water wherever you drilled, so it did not really matter where you put your well. That's why, he concluded, the dowsers got away with it.

But Maria Pazzaglia's son, Roberto studying engineering at Perugia University, reckoned that Luigi had never, never (he stressed the word so that I would understand) never failed yet. When I told Giovanni Filipini this – he had adopted the habit of dropping by to see how the work was progressing – he changed tack. This time he decided the price was wrong: 'Why didn't you tell me what Renato was going to charge? I would have told you you're paying too much. I know a man who would have done it much cheaper. What's more, you should do a deal, if they find no water you only pay half . . . they only get the full price if they find water.'

When Sergio, our surveyor, who supervised the project, turned up, he strongly disagreed that the price was too high, after all, it was the lower of two estimates. For good measure, he formally instructed Renato to drill exactly where we had marked it with a wooden post near the olive grove, and not a centimetre away from that point in any direction.

This was the situation when I arrived a few days later. My trousers were still fluttering on the clothes line in what small breeze there was; the blue and white battered lorry, with the rusting gantry on the back, was still perched precariously at an angle of thirty degrees to the horizontal, and no work had been done.

For three days the lorry sat there, and nothing moved. We went on watering the grass and the plants by hand, looking with less annoyance at the low pressure of the mains water, and not bothering quite as much about the slight chlorine odour that wafted over us when the breeze changed direction. Soon, we assured ourselves the well would be there and we would have plenty of water. Who knows, after the chemical analysis, it might be so pure we could bottle and drink it and, in years to come, start to sell it as the purest Italian mineral water, alongside the oil from the trees in the olive grove.

We called Sergio, our surveyor in Tavernelle, to tell him that Renato still had not arrived. He feigned indignation, as only an Italian professional can feign indignation. He said he would call Renato to hurry him up and he would call us back. Silence. We tried again. He said he would call us back. Silence.

And then, just as in the Bible, on the third day they arrived, Renato and his young sidekick, Mauro. First there was an even bigger lorry. But since it would not go down the side of the land between the wall and the field next door, they had to dump the stuff and go in search of a tractor. I would have thought they would have known this from Renato's first visit. That took two hours. Then, a third man arrived and parked his car in the shade on the other side of the land. He then relieved himself thoughtfully into the laurel hedge, zipped up his blue overall, wiped his brow and walked purposefully towards the lorry that had been parked for a week on the land near the olives. His name turned out to be Luigi, the same as our water diviner's. We took that as a sign. Both men, I noticed, wore thin gold chains round their necks with a small gold crucifix hanging from them. The way they looked at Victoria suggested that the crucifix around the neck did not stop them from idly contemplating the sins of the flesh whenever the opportunity presented itself. But those looks of appreciation are the standard reaction of the Italian male when a woman walks by and may not even register anything more than a reflex action, which has been part of their lives since they were born and told by their mothers that they were God's gift to women and, whatever evidence to the contrary might suggest, were irresistible.

Then the big lorry came back and the tractor was wheeled off; the tubes, drills, old motor-car tyres, buckets and pieces of wood were hauled down to the site. Renato still thought we would be better off putting the well somewhere else. It was not until I saw him manoeuvring the tractor in and out of and around the young olive trees that I realized it meant a great deal more work and effort to put the well where we had indicated.

But then I don't think we had much choice in the matter. If you have land in Umbria you need water. The water from the commune is expensive and not for garden use. If you have sixty olive trees and over an acre and a half of land, then you will need a well. The best advice we got was to find ourselves a water diviner, a *rabdomante* as he is called. Giulio, our gardener, inquired in the village, and the man they all suggested was Luigi Venturini. He was a small man, wiry, and as brown as the soil he worked all his life. He lived with his rather plumper wife, Anna, in a small house down the hill in Casaltondo, with the obligatory flower pots round the door and on the window sills, a small field, with vines and olives, and vegetables growing on every inch of land he could work. He was something of an odd-job man, always to be seen working someone's land, driving a tractor, helping to repair the dirt road that leads up past our house and on up round the bend through the woods to our neighbour Mr Galiotti's house at the top of the hill.

Luigi never said much. He seemed to have a permanent smile on his face but it may have been the way he squinted his eyes against the strong sunlight in summer, and his features had set like that. He would wave when he got to know you. When I say wave, it was more of a movement of the hand in the air than an actual wave. He could be aged anything between late fifties and late sixties. He always seemed to wear the same clothes and a flat hat to keep the sun off.

'He's the best there is,' Giulio Cerboni assured me, 'you know that small lake near Mr Galiotti's house, it was Luigi who found that water, ask anyone around here.' Giulio told me of other wells, other finds of water. But there is a certain etiquette about asking someone to look for water on one's land, Giulio explained. You don't offer him money before he does the work. He will either say yes or no. Luckily, Luigi said 'yes' and turned up one day with a small twig of elm, shaped like a rather large chicken wishbone. He walked the land with that, up and down, until the twig would not stop bucking in his hand, turning upwards as if it wanted to strike him in the chest. Where it moved most was the spot.

To someone from Britain, the idea of placing one's faith in a little old countryman like Luigi, and spending a few thousand pounds on his say-so, seemed rather a large gamble. But at least I could let him try. He turned up unexpectedly when we had our friends, Sergio and Ornella, over for afternoon tea, a habit they liked because, they said, it was so English. It's odd, but back in Britain, I don't think we have ever had anyone over for afternoon tea but such is the fashion for things English in Italy, that they have reinvented the idea, even in a backwater like Umbria, and nothing we can do can dissuade people. I hate to admit it but I think it's a shame it has largely gone out of fashion in England.

Luigi arrived with Giulio who came over and told us conspiratorially to look after our guests and ignore Luigi. He, Giulio, would sort out with Luigi what had to be done. But you can't really ignore a man walking purposefully up and down, hunched over a small twig, to chat about this and that as if he wasn't there. Almost at once Ornella and Sergio guessed what was happening and became as fascinated as we were as to what would happen. Suddenly, Luigi had an audience agog. I worried lest some aura emanated from us, an aura of scepticism which would stop the vibrations or whatever. But all Italians, even water diviners, like an audience. Luigi put on a show for us and, like bees to a honeypot, our guests could not resist, like all Italians, in getting involved in what was going on.

Luigi didn't mind in the least. He went about his business as if it was usual for him to be the centre of attention and to work in front of an audience which chattered, laughed and discussed the wonders of water divining as if it was a diversion put on specially to make afternoon tea a memorable event. Ornella's brother, Sergio, told me of tales he had heard when he was working in Africa, and Ornella's niece, who had unexpectedly arrived with her husband from Sicily and had come along for tea too, said that in Sicily many people had the gift.

While all this babble was going on, Luigi had been quietly walking up and down until he found a spot near the house, the perfect place for a well. We stopped talking, and watched the twig bend up in his hands as he walked across the area from every angle until he had pinpointed the spot. Then the most surprising thing: he got out his fob watch, I think it was silver and, standing hunched over the spot, he let it swing, each movement, he told me, represented a metre in depth . . . he counted a hundred metres . . . much too deep. But, he said, farther down the land, on the same side, near the olives, was another interesting spot. We all trooped down there with him, and once again watched, this time in silence, as the twig twitched quite violently. He struggled to hold it in place. Once again he took out the silver watch and counted the swings. Fifty metres down, said Luigi, there is water.

I asked to try with the twig but nothing happened. We all tried, but it was only Ornella who had the same reaction as Luigi, and over the same spot. Until that moment, she hadn't known that she had the power of water divining. Nobody else got the smallest reaction. Ornella moved to the first place that

Luigi had spotted and again she got a reaction but none of the rest of us got the merest hint of any movement.

A book I found on the subject by Tom Williamson, subtitled *New Light on an Ancient Art*, says that though the Romans practised many forms of divination, dowsing was unknown to them. But I wonder whether the Etruscans, who lived here before the Romans and who were well known for their divination as well as for their use of water to irrigate their highly productive farms, may have known about it. Williamson reckons, that the earliest references to dowsing come from northern Germany in the fifteenth century and, a surprise to me, it's not just water but metal that the dowser can find. Williamson reckons there is almost scientific proof that dowsing works. Mind you, he ruins the thesis for me by trying to link some dowsing to crop circles. However, the people in question get some small reaction either to sound waves or electro-magnetic vibrations. The book is quite explicit: not only water can be found but also metals and oil. There are old prints which show German dowsers at work in the seventeenth and eighteenth centuries. A French scientist has made a serious study of it, concluding that it does work and that dowsers are to be trusted. But even though the book was reassuring, I still wondered whether one should hazard so much money on a small, I almost wrote pint-sized, Umbrian water diviner, who accepted the 50,000 lire (£25) I gave him at Giulio's suggestion.

There were many considerations to take into account. First, you had to trust the *rabdomante*. Luigi had lived in the place all his life, he was still being recommended by all and sundry, so he must have done something to deserve his reputation. So, on balance, I think I could accept his word that there was water under the soil. Yet, intriguingly, when he had walked over the septic tank which was buried not far from the spot where he said there was water, the twig had not moved at all. It must be a very clever twig that can tell the difference between sewage and pure water.

Then there's the question of the depth at which the water lies. This is crucial to the cost of the whole operation and thus one's economic peace of mind. But, as everyone said, you had to trust Luigi's word for that too. So the second problem was whether the swinging watch really worked, for I could find no mention of that in my book on dowsing. The opinion of Renato, as we knew, would be to drill somewhere else but all he did was give you an estimate of so much per metre. So did you stop at 50 metres and say no more or, like roulette, did you let the chips ride on the number 50 hoping it would come up a winner, or did you prepare yourself and go for broke, letting Renato and his small band of well-diggers pound the earth with their pile-driving device until they hit water? And would they be interested in doing the work, if you told them there was a limit to the amount you would spend? And could they leave a 50-metre-deep hole next to your olives without something terrible happening, like a landslip when the rains came?

Giovanni Filipini, on the next hill, is of the school that believes that, if you drill far enough down, you'll hit water anyway. But then the cost at £60 a metre means that it could become prohibitively expensive, so could you stop after three days and say, 'Bad luck, Luigi was wrong, here's £3,500.' I'm not a company like British Petroleum who can write off exploration costs before tax. A dry well, and I still had to pay for the privilege of Renato and his two companions drilling a hundred or more metres down into my land.

And there were other problems to take into account. At Sunday lunch, some friends in Badia, a few miles away, told us scare stories of the couple who dug a well, but did not analyse the water. It was polluted: it ruined their vines and poisoned them, though not fatally. And another chap, a professor of chemistry from Perugia University, said with all the seriousness of an Italian intellectual, that the water table was falling and it might well be that the well would be dry within years if not months. So even if you found the water, you might still not get your money's worth.

Stacked against all the arguments for not risking your money on a hole in the ground, is the incontrovertible need for water in a country where the summer months are largely rain-free, and very hot. All my classical guides to growing vines and olives, and anything else for that matter, stress that water is what makes the difference. Not that I really needed to be told. In one of my favourite French films, *Jean de Florette*, Gérard Depardieu slowly dies as he struggles to bring water to his plot, because Yves Montand has blocked up the well that rightly belongs to him. That part of France is not unlike my part of Italy, idyllic in the pictures, but pitiless and backbreaking unless you have the know-how to create a garden paradise. True, I hadn't had to hire a donkey and walk miles to a nearby spring. But the dribbles of rather sickly smelling chlorinated water, which oozed from the hosepipe attached to the mains supply, meant that we spent every morning starting at six squirting the liquid over the parched soil for more hours than were good for either of us or our relationship.

My first-century friend, Columella, whose advice I had followed in planting my olive grove had this to say: 'A landowner [forgive the affectation but that's how the Romans saw anyone with a piece of land bought and paid for] should make sure that there is a never-failing spring either within the steading or brought in from outside ... if running water is wanted, make a search for a well close by but not too deep for the hoisting of the water, and not bitter nor brackish in taste.'

Most people broke the rules and watered plants with water

from the commune, thus becoming *abusivi* (abusers, law breakers), but it didn't do to be too obvious. It was not unknown for the occasional busybody to walk past even at six in the morning to ask you where your well was.

There was, however, another possibility. Again we go back to Columella who wrote, 'If the well fails, and if scanty hope of veins of water compels it, have a large cistern built for people and ponds for cattle; this rainwater is uncommonly good if it is conveyed through earthern pipes into a covered cistern.' There's no doubt about it, when the rains do come in Italy they can be torrential, dropping gallons of water on you in a matter of hours. But the thought of covering the roof with pipes (in the hardware shop, they were plastic and coloured a very bright, disconcerting orange) leading to barrels all over the place, was too much. No, it had to be a well.

So gamble it might be, expensive it might be, but there was nothing for it but to trust Luigi and his gift. It was Maria Pazzaglia who summed up best what we would need – good luck. She used the old Italian phrase: *in bocca al lupo*, 'in the wolf's mouth'. I just hoped we wouldn't get bitten. I went back to London that year determined to take on extra freelance work, to amass what threatened to be a small fortune to pay for my own running water, hoping against hope that it was not bitter or brackish in taste. And that Luigi's watch told the time in metres accurately. It didn't bear thinking about if he was, say, five or ten metres slow.

But, taking the decision, risky though it was, was the easy part. It took eleven months before that blue and white lorry with the drilling platform on the back was dumped one July day in the olive grove. First, as with everything else, we had to get permission.

We left the paperwork to our surveyor, Sergio Sargentini. He said he trusted Luigi, our water diviner, but if we wanted he could get another chap along just to cross-check that there was water where Luigi's elm twig had indicated. Inevitably, forms had to be filled in and a small sum of money changed hands, in the legal fashion, to buy the stamp duty. In total some 75,000 lire went on four red and blue and one yellow and pink stamps, plus the overstamping with the coat of arms of the communes. First, the forms went to our local commune, Città della Pieve but, because it was a well, another stamp had to be bought and it went up to provincial level, and so ended up in Perugia. Finally, the piece of paper came back and informed me that under the regional law number 9 of January 1979, 'following the advice of the technical council of the regional health authority', I was allowed to drill a well on my land which was part number 464 on the tax register, file number 14. But, having taken the best part of a year to get, they only gave me six months for the work to start, otherwise the permission was withdrawn and I would have to start all over again.

Then, after waiting and watching the lorry in the olive grove, suddenly it was all activity: Renato turned up with Luigi and Mauro and started to level the land around the point that Luigi Venturini, the water diviner, had suggested. Renato's employees were a strange couple: Luigi was quite old, haggard even, with one tooth left in the front of his upper jaw. He was the one who had the disconcerting habit of relieving himself publicly from time to time. He wore a blue and white, rather limp, cotton hat, the same colours as the lorry, but I think that was just happenstance. His job was to lower and lift the lever on the back of the lorry that sent the pile-driver down through the earth, to what we hoped was the water vein fifty metres down. Mauro was much younger, wore a white singlet, blue overalls and white plimsolls – again, I think the colour co-ordination with the lorry was simple coincidence.

It's an odd process, drilling for water in Umbria. Once the rig was put in place, a huge piece of metal, more or less star-shaped and about ten metres long, was pounded into the ground. After a time, a metal collar was put round the top of the hole and water was poured in to soften up the soil. Then, another piece of metal, again ten metres in length, was manoeuvred into place and sent down the hole, to bring out the mud and slurry which fills its hollow inside. This is then pulled out and up-ended into a shallow basin which has been dug near the drilling rig. Slowly, a muddy lake starts to form and the action is endlessly repeated for hours on end: first, the pile-driver, then the scoop, then more water, then the pile-driver, then the scoop and then more water. I hate to think how much water was being used from the local authority to ease the passage of our pile-driver. Giovanni Filipini, who seems to have made a study of wells, wondered why we didn't just drill for water, as it would take half the time. Since we had been given no say in the method of well-making, the question was academic.

On the first day they made a depth of seventeen metres. The next morning no Mauro, no Luigi. We worried. But not for long. At eleven they arrived without a word of explanation and started work. By mid-afternoon they were down to thirty metres. By the end of the day, a Friday, they were down to forty metres. Soon we would know whether Luigi was right about the depth he expected the water to be – we were just ten metres away from his estimated fifty. Giovanni was still unimpressed by Luigi. He had been watching the progress from the top of his hill, through binoculars. As I was to discover, drilling for water was a communal event, not to be kept to oneself. Everyone wanted to be in on the affair.

The most frustrating thing was that I had to go back to London for work and so I wouldn't be there when water was struck. That should happen on Monday. 'It's a marvellous moment,' said Giovanni, my self-appointed well consultant, 'I wouldn't miss it for anything, even though it's not my well.'

Needless to say, the team decided to keep us waiting just a little longer: they did not turn up for another two days. So we were left in a state of suspended animation ... so near to Luigi's estimated depth but as far as ever, because no work was being done. Victoria, alone once more, no doubt with a pair of my trousers on the washing line for reassurance, went on watering in the old way, very early in the morning.

Finally they came back and, at fifty-one metres, they got the first traces of water. Luigi's elm twig had done its stuff. Even Giovanni was impressed that he should be so close. But the disappointment was that there was no gusher that sprung from the earth. No sudden rush of clear cold pure water spraying over the land with everyone dancing in the shower. What actually happens is that the drill bit comes up clean, no more mud clinging to the end. As it pushes through the vein, so it comes up cleaner. They pushed on for another ten metres or more, so that the pump could be lowered down below the water level, and then pumped up the water into the pipes and out over the land. And here was an omen if ever there was one, the name of the company that made the submersible pump had been reduced to three letters – BBC. With a name like that the pump had to be something you could trust. I was on the same wavelength, so to speak.

There was one magical moment reserved for Victoria, not for me, by Renato, who took her to the well head, a hole barely thirty centimetres in diameter and, with the aid of a small mirror, managed to shine a sunbeam down fifty metres plus, until it hit the water down below.

Then suddenly it was all over, the top was put on and the pump cable was linked up to the electricity supply. In a shallow ditch the water pipe was laid to feed the water to two sets of taps at the front and back of the house. The earth was pushed back into place and tidied up and Renato and his team were gone to their next well.

We bought some more tubing. We also invested in a couple more sprinklers with heads that turn under the pressure of the water until a full circle of soil is showered with a fine mist, creating lovely rainbows when the sunlight catches them. So, through the orange-red plastic tube, via a rainbow-coloured spray, the grass turned a deep luscious green within a week. Everything rallied: the laurel was beginning to shoot out young leaves, the trees produced new delicately green foliage and the whole place stood out sharply when we walked to the top of the hill and looked down on our handiwork. The travel books call Umbria, the 'green heart of Italy', but only if you've got a well. So we did our bit for the tourist trade, while the rest of Umbria, where there was little water being used, turned browner by the day. Our house stood out like an oasis in the desert.

'Use as much water as you can,' advised Giulio and everyone else who stopped by to see the water. 'The more you use, the stronger the vein will become, it'll pull the water down to it, and give you a good flow,' said Giovanni. When Maria Pazzaglia and her husband, Mario, who sustain us in so many ways, stopped on their way up to their vines with a huge barrel of water from their well down below, their first word was 'Complimenti', as if we had done all the work. Our neighbours and Maria's cousins had been phoning from Aosta, where they spend the summer with their children, for news of the well. Maria had called specially to tell them we had struck water. The man who has the digger, whom we spoke to on the day we looked at the house for the first time, climbed down from his driving seat one morning (no easy matter for a heavily built man in his sixties) and shook my hand. '*Complimenti*,' he said and, like Giulio, our gardener, remarked that we were richer than people who just had money.

Soon we got the hang of just setting the sprinklers, or *irrigatori* in Italian, in the right places. They are ingenious little bits of machinery: the jet of water is interrupted by a piece of metal which, as it flicks back and forth, forces the head round in a circle; after a time, a spring catch hits a piece of adjustable wire, making the spring change direction, and round the head goes in the opposite direction. How anyone thought it up, let alone patented it, I don't know. For all I know it might be the standard piece of irrigating kit in the world. But the clicking sound it makes, like a clock going very fast, is one of the most comforting you can hear in the middle of a drought such as we had that first year of the well.

Apart from adding to our range of implements, the well also added to our vocabulary: the grass or the land had to be *bagnato*, bathed in water, and when it was *molto bagnato*, had a deep bath. You just kept the soil moist with half an hour a day: it must be done in the morning on the vegetables, because the spring water was cold and that was when the soil was at its coolest. As for the olives, only the younger trees needed some watering, especially after you had loosened the soil round the roots, so that the damp and the manure from the animals' stalls would sink down to the roots to do maximum good. As the Latin writers had said, the more you give to your olives, the more they will repay you.

The effects of water very quickly became obvious. The most hang-dog looking plant would perk up on day one, begin to radiate a kind of green lustre by day two and, on day three, tiny shoots would appear as the beneficial effects of water aplenty took hold. The tomato plants began to sprout and the eight or nine rather weedy-looking things, which we had planted back in April that first year, were starting to become laden with fruit after a week or two of heavy watering before the sun was properly up or there was any heat in the day. I can't explain why, rising around sun-up, to a clear fresh morning, it was bliss to pad downstairs and, at the flick of a switch, watch the water first bubble, then spurt, out of the irrigators, arching over the plants, the trees or the grass, and shower everything. Chaucer wrote in the Prologue to *The Canterbury Tales* about the sweet showers of April: 'When April with its sweet showers has inspired every wood and field . . .' In Umbria, when the well came in, it was like April every morning that first summer. And, even now, the idea that we have fifty metres below the surface of our olive grove a stream we can call our own, giving us fresh water whenever we want it, is a very comforting thought. Now anything was possible in the garden and on the land.

We got very ambitious for the garden, the *orto* as the Italians call it and, like Giovanni on the hill, or Maria, or Sergio, we too would grow not just tomatoes but courgettes, egg plants and a whole range of vegetables. Dreaming of such things is part of the charm of investing part of your life in Umbria but, while Goethe dreamed of a land where the lemon trees grow, he didn't have to plant them. Gardening is reality, as we had already discovered. Gardening without enough water was almost impossible, so the well gave us a huge new lease of life and allowed us to become even more ambitious in our plans for what we might grow. But a well is more than running water. The well fixed us more firmly in the community and tied us more lovingly to the place, than anything we had done in the first five years . . . the house, the olives, everything . . . The well, somehow, was a declaration of intent, of staying put for as far ahead as we could see.

The water, however, even though it came up sparkling from

fifty metres below the soil, cold and clear, could have been dangerous. So there remained one last chore. Once the water had been drawn for a few weeks, I had to take a small jar of it to Panicale for analysis. The water looked good and I did not wait until we had the official clearance to taste it, tentatively, I must say, just in case it was bad. But it tasted sweet, not a bit salty. And it tasted better than the only other well water I had drunk. This was in an old hunting lodge near Cortona, which the American journalist and mafia expert, Claire Stirling, and her husband have had for many years. Her wonderfully cool old house set in a clearing, way up a track in the middle of a forest, miles from any neighbours, is said to have been a Medici hunting lodge. It would have been prohibitively expensive to run the local commune's water up there, so Claire has her well water pumped into her house and you get it through a tap just over the sink. She says she finds the tap water in Rome tastes bad in comparison. I prefer mine, of course, but then she would say the same about her well no doubt.

So we watered everything in sight, every day for a few weeks, before we went one morning to what's called USL in Panicale. Panicale is a sleepy little place that hasn't changed much down the centuries, nor has it attracted too much urban sprawl around its thick walls. It has a few brief claims on the historian's time, Boldrino a famous mercenary or *condottiere* was born there, and there was a painter Masolino, who was active around a few decades before my chum Perugino made his name. Otherwise Panicale bides its time, waiting for another local hero to emerge as it knows one day he will. Meanwhile, its contribution to modern-day civilization is a water-testing facility and, luckily for us, the man who is in charge of such things in the little town hall comes from our village and recognized us.

'Leave it to me,' he said, taking the half filled-up forms, and starting work on them himself. 'It's the house up near Galiot-ti's, isn't it, *bellissima* . . .' And asking us to give him half an hour, said he would have everything done for us. 'After all we're both strangers in this town, we must help each other.'

Out into the sunlight we went, and popped to the church next door to the town hall to see a Perugino and a Masolino, for good measure. I made some notes, wandered round the town, had a cup of coffee near Boldrino's old house, and went back and got my certificate.

It's this combination of then and now that is so entrancing and that makes one, if one is not careful, a bit of an Umbria bore. It was my colleague, John Humphrys on *Today*, who put me in my place. John has a few acres in Wales, where he goes to get some peace so, as one part-time rustic to another, I had kept him informed about the progress of the well. I thought he was interested. But when at last I told him early one morning that we had struck water and that we now had our own well, John, as if he were interviewing a politician interrupted rather brusquely and said:

'Peter you don't have a well, you have a bore hole.'

For a good friend, I thought he put rather too much empha-sis on the word 'bore'.

6 Wild Boar and Wine-Making

SOMETIMES IN THESE EARLY YEARS, no matter how much we would wish it otherwise, we can only be spectators at some of the annual rituals in Umbria. The *vendemmia*, the grape harvest, is such a time at the moment and will continue to be so until we feel brave enough to plant our own vines for wine-making. But that can only come when we spend the greater part of the year here.

The only vine we have is the one that covers the pergola and produces heavy, dark, purple fruit which is for the table, not for the bottle, and which we cut as and when we want to eat it once the grapes are ripe enough. When we shut up the house in the autumn, we cut down what fruit remains and leave it in the garden store room in separate bunches, on paper on wood, and it is often still good enough to eat in January when we come back for the winter break. But the real *vendemmia*, the one that produces the wines of the region, comes in Umbria once the nights are beginning to draw in, and the occasional south wind, the sirocco, blows warm and humid air across from Africa, sometimes as a gentle caress, other times bending everything in its path into the most alarming angles.

There's no announcement on the television or radio that now is the time to gather in the grapes. Down in the *mezzo-giorno*, it's early September, farther north, in Lombardy, later. Here in central Italy, early October seems to be the average. Suddenly, it seems, the moment has arrived and friends and neighbours work in groups along the vine rows. Once we were spectators to two separate rituals at this time of the year and on the same day – the wine harvest and a boar hunt,

It was the second Sunday in October, a warm sunny day, with everything looking unusually green after the torrential rain of the previous week. And the warmth was lulling the plants and trees into believing that maybe it was spring rather than autumn, so tiny fresh green shoots had started to appear on the persimmon tree, while some of the slow-moving olive trees had produced a few new curled young leaves. Even at seven o'clock in the morning, it was warm enough to go outside and savour the clean air without needing to wear a jacket or a sweater. These are moments to treasure in the year, because October mornings can be very fresh sometimes and by November you begin to worry about what the occasional frost might do to the olive trees.

Once outside that morning, the happy sound of Maria Pazzaglia's family already at work on their vines drifted down the hill: all of them were there, carrying white plastic containers, which had once held paint or plaster or somesuch from the local ironmongers and paint shop. As they moved along each row of vines, snipping this bunch and that and dropping them into the bucket, the conversation never flagged. Mario, seated on his tractor and towing a trailer, was rounding up the full buckets and dumping the contents, stalks and all, into square, dark red plastic boxes (*cassa* is the Italian word, meaning drawer). At the end of the day, I was told, they had filled ninety-two drawers, which would make quite a few litres of wine. The drawers were stacked one on top of the other. He didn't seem to mind if a few grapes were crushed in the rush to get the boxes on to the trailer and down to the garage where he had his wine-making equipment and, where, only weeks before, Maria had been busy boiling the tomatoes to make the sauce that would be bottled in a variety of shapes and sizes to see her through the winter as a good sauce for pasta or meat.

All the generations were at work and all branches of the family. Our closest neighbours, the Mancinis, were also down from Aosta to gather up the grapes and, a month or so later, their olive crop. The first of their harvest meals would be cooked on a small gas-ring which provided vast quantities from only two pots, yet they were as tasty as anything that came from modern, bigger stoves. Mind you, she still made *bruschetta* by toasting the bread in front of their open fire.

Apart from the Mancinis, who had seen more harvests on this land than anyone else in the party, both Maria's sons were there, and Luigi, the *rabdomante*, and his wife Anna, and another cousin, whose name I never found out but who lived not far away and who always nodded a greeting whenever our paths crossed.

The grape harvest is a team and family effort and works on the unwritten law of 'you pick my grapes, and I'll pick yours'. So when one group's fruit is in, they then move to another vineyard and help out there. Whoever's vines are being picked, provides the food, lots of it, washed down with the last of the previous year's vintage, still fresh and light tasting like the best of the young new beaujolais that used to be in fashion in Britain a few years ago.

But that Sunday morning another sound imposed itself on

the enthusiastic conversations of the family harvesting the grape. This sound was less peaceable. It was the raucous noise of men shouting plus the intermittent sound of gunshot. Sounds in the hills around the village are deceptive: sometimes you can hear a conversation as if it is happening beneath your window, the rattle of a tractor and plough as if it is your field that is being worked . . . and yet you see no one. Like some vast, natural echo chamber, you can never tell exactly where the sound is coming from, or how near or far. But this new sound reminded me that October means not only the vine harvest, but the hunting season as well.

Until that morning, most of the hunting had taken place unseen and deep in the woods higher up the hills. We had been woken up by the sound of gunfire early in the mornings during the season and sometimes seen a hunter with his dog walking down the hill with his rifle slung over his shoulder. Maria's eldest son, Stefano was a hunter too, and he often walked along the side of our land down towards the woods where the hares and rabbits provide good sport and good food for the pot. Maria told us that one day she would give us some hare cooked in the traditional manner – a stew of herbs and vegetables, with garlic and wine thrown in for good measure. So, until this particular morning, I had always imagined the Umbrian hunter as a man and his dog pitted against the speed and courage of a single animal. A fairly equal contest with fair play on both sides. This morning was to be a rude awakening from that naïve dream. There we were, going quietly about the autumnal business of weeding the terrace, applying some grass killer between the tufa flagstones and between times watching the progress of the grape pickers up on the ridge when, all of a sudden, a convoy of half a dozen cars rounded the corner and parked here and there alongside the road. Eighteen hunters – I counted them out – leapt from the vehicles, all sporting battle fatigues, green wellington boots and cartridges slung around their waists or over their shoulders.

'Did you see it?' called out the tallest and the thinnest man among them. He was the most lugubrious-looking man I had ever seen in Italy – concave chest, a drooping moustache and dark, hollowed eyes.

'See what?' I shouted back.

'The *cinghiale*, the wild boar . . .' he said in a voice which now recognized that he had foreigners to deal with. 'It came this way, we've wounded it . . .'

But before he could finish a shout went up: 'Here, here . . .' and a babble of dialect words which neither of us could understand filled the air. Half the team rushed off and the tall man came up to the house and asked for some water. When I told him I had never seen a wild boar before, he immediately invited us to join the final moves in the morning's hunt. As we talked and started to walk down the hill, I saw pinned to his chest a heart-shaped badge, with a boar in front of a red cross, and the words round the edge of the badge: 'Red Cross of Città della Pieve, Wild Boar Squadron'. Others, I noticed when we joined them, had similar badges and a few had white heart-shaped badges, with the words: 'Boar Squadron of Moiano'. But it was the military outfits that really struck home . . . here I was surrounded by a group of Italians who must have looked much like the partisans who would have appeared in these self-same hills fifty years before, when the Allies were pushing north towards Florence.

Even the young boy, hardly more than ten, was in complete combat fatigues, with a knife, big as a bowie knife, hanging ostentatiously from his belt. Cartridge bandoliers criss-crossed his small chest and he was as flushed in the face from the chase and as breathless with excitement and effort as the rest.

They were all on an adrenalin-induced high. The early nineteenth-century English author, R.S. Surtees said that hunting is 'the image of war without the guilt, and only five and twenty per cent of its danger'. Given the numbers and the artillery involved, he probably over-estimated the danger to the modern Umbrian hunter by a factor of at least twenty per cent. Mind you, it's a well known fact that in Italy there are more accidents, many of them fatal when the hunting season starts, than should be the case, and folklore has it that often it's the way a betrayed husband settles the score with the hunting companion who seduced his wife. But the group that October Sunday morning seemed much more interested in the boar they had been tracking, and in enjoying each other's company, for there to be any bad blood between the hunters.

The wounded animal had been located deep in a patch of wild woodland between the fields of vine and olives. Most of the trees are wild oak, and most of them in October are heavy with acorns said to be the boar's favourite food when not stealing grapes. Many Italians, who are partial to boar, say that a young acorn-fed boar is some of the best meat you can eat. The animal was immediately put out of its misery with a single shot behind the ear and the small Land Rover, the only suitable vehicle in what was a convoy of family saloons, had gone to drag it out. Part of the myth of the hunt is the idea of danger. I was told that it takes at least a dozen men to hunt together for safety: there are tales galore, though I suspect largely apocryphal, of wounded boars turning on the group hunting it and killing some of its attackers before they can kill it. But the odds in the modern world of that must be about the same as the bull in the Spanish *corrida* surviving the picadors' attentions and the skill of the matador. It does happen but only rarely, and, when it does, it adds to the legend of danger and helps to reinforce some masculine need to measure one's courage against the odds. This was just another side of *bella figura* in Italian life. Unlike Britain, where hunting is largely the preserve of the rich, hunting in Italy is almost solely the province of the working classes and mainly rural ones at that. There is a move to try to stop it and the rules are made tighter every year, with huge posters on walls and notice boards, and outside town halls. In 1990, there was a referendum to decide whether to ban hunting altogether but, when the hunters with impeccable logic refrained from voting, they ensured that not enough people took part to form a quorum and so the referendum failed.

'It's big, a hundred kilos,' said the boss, 'and it's male.'

Someone identified as Maurizio had given it the *coup de grâce*, so to Maurizio went the spoils, but they all expected to be sharing the roast and stuffed results for the next few days. My friend Sergio Contini explained, a few days later when I had told him of the hunt, that the general rule was that those who hunted together tended to share the kill equally between them: 'They hunt as a team and they eat as a team.' But it all depends, local restaurants like Da Bruno, the best in Città della Pieve, know their customers like to eat boar when it's in season and, two days after the hunt on our land, we too were sampling boar in a thick wine and tomato sauce, the chunks of the dark meat as tender as anything. 'Not a gramme of fat, you see,' said Sergio, 'that's why it's so good.'

Two men ran up the hill shouting, 'Here it comes ...' Behind them, the Land Rover changing down through the gears pushed its way past them, and behind it came the boar, its two back legs tied together by a thick rope which had been latched on to the towing hook of the Land Rover. It was massive, though a hundred kilos was rather an exaggeration, with brown-grey harsh hair all over its body; I couldn't see the two sharp teeth but it had two small bullet holes, one in the side of its head and one behind its big flapping ear. There was hardly any blood, which surprised me, and the eyes were open, staring out sightlessly but with an air of surprise.

'It's eaten a whole line of my vines,' said one of the men, indicating the field next to us, which I passed on my way down the hill every day, 'a whole line of them, goddammit.'

Maurizio's car was one of those rather old Fiats with a small roof rack and two men lifted the boar on to the roof and tied it down with some difficulty. Then, all of a sudden, it was handshakes all round and the quick explanation from the boss that now they must hunt in another part of the countryside for they were only allowed to kill one boar in one patch. I counted the eighteen hunters back in – they hadn't lost anybody – and the eight cars slowly drove off in procession behind Maurizio's venerable Fiat van, with the heaving body and the bouncing head of the boar on the roof.

Boar hunting goes back through history. It's popular all over Europe and used to be great sport in Britain too a few hundred years ago. In the Middle Ages it was, like most hunting, done as much to protect the crops as to find food to eat. These great ugly and lumbering animals have an amazing turn of speed when they need it and can shift up through the gears and leave the hunters far behind. But the boar, because of its looks, also creates a particular atmosphere and during the witch hunts of the Middle Ages, the boar was sometimes seen as the devil incarnate. We have an old print in the house of a boar from Cap Verde, huge and ugly with lumps on the body, curled horns on the nose and great teeth out of the side of the mouth. It's the ugliness and brute strength combined with the speed and survival instinct that makes it seem a worthy prey in the hunters' minds, even if today they career around the countryside in a motorcade, armed to the limit with enough ammunition to kill all the wild boars in Umbria.

How different were the boar hunts of the original inhabitants of these hills, covered then as now with the wild oak and the dense scrub in which the boars could hide and make their homes safe from the hunter. The Etruscans, ever an elegant people, are said to have used their flutes to great effect. Aelian, writing in the third century AD reports (and here I'm using the translation in the Loeb Classical library, *De natura animalium* by A.F. Scholfield 1959):

> There is an Etruscan story current which says that the wild boars and stags in that country are caught by using nets and hounds as is the usual manner of hunting, but that music plays a part, and an even larger part, in the struggle . . . they set out the nets and other hunting gear that ensnare the animals in a circle, and a man proficient on the pipes stands there and tries his utmost to play a rather soft tune, avoiding any shriller note, but playing the sweetest melodies possible. The quiet and the stillness easily carry the sound abroad; the music streams up to the heights, and into the ravines and thickets – in a word in every lair and resting place of these animals. Now at first when the sound penetrates to their ears it strikes them with terror and fills them with dread, and then an unalloyed and irresistible delight in the music takes hold of them . . . and beneath the wizardry of the music they come and fall into the snares, overpowered by the melody.

In the fifteenth century, the music seems to have disappeared but still the hunters go mob handed. There's a marvellous picture by that strange painter Piero di Cosimo, an eccentric if ever there was one. He never weeded his garden and lived only on hard-boiled eggs but, apart from a few obligatory Madonnas, this almost exact contemporary of my friend Perugino produced a curious picture which is in the Metropolitan Museum of Art in New York. It's a hunting scene of unmitigated slaughter. Piero di Cosimo felt more for animals than human beings, some of his contemporaries believed. There are mythical beasts, centaurs, one of which is playing the Pipes of Pan (a nod in the direction of ancient Etruria where music was used, I wonder?), men heaving huge staves, animals being strangled. A picture of the 'universal warfare between men and animals', is how the great American Renaissance scholar Professor Frederick Hartt described it. Well, those days are long gone in many countries, though they still exist to a degree in Italy during the hunting season. In the twentieth century, there is no music, only raucous shouts as the hunters try to scare the animal into the open, no nets to try to snare the animal before it is speared or clubbed to death, but now a quick aim with the hunting rifle and the beast is brought down. But still the need to hunt in numbers remains, with nothing to fear but fear itself.

What was striking, however, in the hunt I witnessed was the team spirit which the eighteen men and the one boy exuded . . . all had had a hand in the kill even though it was Maurizio who claimed the shot that brought down the beast. It was an all-male ritual too: Victoria's presence, though not resented, felt odd and the men were unusually shy with her, preferring to talk to me and explain where and how they had tracked the boar. In more normal circumstances, Italians make a point of talking to the woman rather than the man as they show off in front of her and pay exaggerated compliments. This, they seemed to say, was man's work and man's world. The camaraderie also explained why the hunters club, which met during the winter in the house down the hill, was such a closed world. We once asked Maria whether anyone could go there but she said no, only members of the *squadra*. The team that hunts together, kills together and eats together. It may not be politically correct in the northern hemisphere but in my part of Italy it's the way it's been for generations and will be for many more. One estimate I read (in Peter Nichols's *Italia, Italia*) reckoned that every year 600,000 men put 'on their green jackets, load their double-barrelled shotguns and fire almost at anything that moves . . . in 1971,' the author continued, '50 million animals died and 200 million birds. I doubt whether the figures have changed much despite the growing mood against hunting and a proliferation of notices stressing that this or that parcel of land is "Private Property. Hunting is Forbidden".'

My land is open, there are no fences or barriers around it and it is set in the middle of a state-protected parkland, so the hunters are free to come and go and, indeed, when we bought the house, the big empty room in the centre, now our sitting room, had often been used as a shelter for hunting groups, lighting a fire and maybe roasting a rabbit or even a baby boar, leaving empty cartridges and Perroni beer cans. On one of the few occasions when I went to lunch with ex-patriots, I remember fanatical anti-bloodsport guests fulminating about the slaughter and the fact that one's land was never private. I'm not sure I like hunting but somehow it seems hard for a foreigner to have a view about something that happens in the country in which he has decided to have a home.

But one more thought on the hunt: it was another ex-patriot, Matthew Spender in his book on life in neighbouring Tuscany, who pointed out that what the Umbrian hunters killed that morning was probably not even a native breed. The boar that the Etruscans killed did not breed as fast and as furiously as was necessary to keep up with the annual slaughter, so after the war, boars from Hungary were introduced, with breeding proclivities akin to rabbits (another favourite target), so much so that the native boar no longer exists. Mind you, some go after the wild pig, the pink cousin of the dark brown boar and, just as *cinghiale*, wild boar, is often on the menu, more often there is *porchetta*, the famous roast stuffed pig of Umbria.

Every Wednesday is market day in Castiglione del Lago. The narrow streets are lined down one side with stall after stall, selling cooking pots, plants, bedlinen, clothes but there is one stall, usually just outside the main gate, which does a roaring trade. A large man, almost boarlike in shape and aspect, serves up hefty chunks of roast stuffed pork, sometimes between bread, sometimes on its own and wrapped in greaseproof paper, for the hungry shoppers and tradespeople. Get there early on Wednesday when the meat is best and the choice is bigger . . . he's usually sold out by lunchtime.

One of the first small gifts Giancarlo, the agent, gave me as we completed on the house, was a traditional cookbook, printed on brown cardboard to give it an historic feel. *Umbria in Bocca*, 'Umbria in Your Mouth', I suppose is the literal translation. Giancarlo had noted my liking for food early on and was always trying to find out how this or that dish was cooked. *Umbria in Bocca* has what it claims is the authentic recipe for roast pork and no doubt this would be what those Sunday-morning marksmen would want to happen to their catch:

Take a wild mountain pig weighing fifty kilos and fed on acorns. On festive occasions peasants cut the pig's abdomen lengthwise, then hang the pig so as to let its blood drip, which takes a whole night at least. Then they remove the entrails that are first washed, cut into pieces, and half-cooked with abundant fennel, cloves of garlic, pepper and salt, and then used to stuff the pig . . . after sewing up the pig, they then cook it for three or four hours in a hot oven with a wood fire . . . when cooked, add more wood to make the skin gold and crackling.'

That's the long and ritual way. Beth Romer, who has lived for many years with her Egyptologist husband in a wild part of Tuscany just north of our area, has a much simpler recipe. In her book *The Tuscan Year*, she describes the cooking of her neighbour, Silvana Cerotti. Silvana cuts the meat into chunks, and washes it, then puts it into a pan with some chopped garlic and some sage leaves that have been stewing in olive oil. When the meat has been sealed on all sides, she adds a large glass of white wine, and goes on cooking slowly until it is ready. Simple country fare which, Ms Romer says, gives boar meat tenderness and tastiness. It was a similar recipe we had in the local restaurant, two days after the kill on our land. So did the Red Cross Boar hunting team of Città della Pieve sell it on to Bruno at the restaurant? Maybe, but I prefer to think it was another boar: I'd be too squeamish to enjoy the flesh of an animal that I had seen killed and carted away in such an unceremonious fashion.

As I say, though, we are but spectators to all this at the moment. All we experienced was the shouting, the sudden appearance of the dead animal and its equally sudden disappearance as the convoy moved off, at high speed, to drive in triumph through the villages and back to base, with the weight of the beast and its toughness growing with each re-telling of that successful Sunday morning hunt.

Though I've thought a lot about the affair since then, the whole incident had lasted but half an hour. As soon as the last car disappeared round the corner, we turned to walk back up the hill to the house. Unknown to us, the grape pickers had finished the lines of vines up on the brow of the hill and so we came across the Pazzaglias picking their way along a row of vines at the Mancinis' house, still talking and laughing. Mario called down to us to come and taste the grapes – you don't refuse such an invitation – so we went nibbling our way through the smallest yet fruitiest and sweetest grapes I have ever eaten . . .

'Will it be a good year?'

'Of course, less fruit this year, but better fruit . . . it's always the way . . . too much fruit, not enough quality and the wine is not so good either.'

Everyone it seemed that Sunday was out in the fields picking the grapes. All of them reported that their fruit was as good as any in the past few years, less of it, because of the dry summer, but just enough rain in the final weeks to give it a last boost of sweetness and sugar. Like hunting, wine-making had undergone immense changes. The Greeks and Romans trod the vines and had teams of slaves to help them in their tasks: the modern Italian vintner with his smallholding now has all the modern machinery he could want.

Sergio Contini showed us what us he had in his garage, because his wine was already made and bottled by the time we got there on Tuesday of that week. Sergio took me through the process, in his fast and slurred Roman accent, which I find so hard to follow. . . . but I'll try to report verbatim what he told me:

'When you've collected the grapes and put them in the boxes, you bring them down to the first machine, which is the *sgranatrice*, which takes the grapes off the stalks and crushes them a little to let the juice, the must out, but there's fruit as well. This we pipe into the *torchio*, which presses the fruit more and more. It's got a handle at the top which you turn so as to squeeze the fruit juice through the slats of wood at the side. The juice falls down into a dish and then away into what we call the *botte* [cask] . . . now, this must be very clean. You leave the juice for say twenty-four hours, and then you give it a stir. Then you let it 'boil' [the verb he used was *bollire* which means to boil, but in this sense obviously means to ferment]. After seven or eight days you then take a small sample to the local wine co-operative, for analysis. The analysis will tell you what needs to be done . . . for example, if it's too acid, you might need to add some *bisolfito* [bisulphite] or, in some circumstances, some bicarbonate of soda, then you leave it for another few days, say fifteen, before you carry out what's called the *sfacciatura*. This is how you get rid of the impurities in the wine, all the bad stuff sinks

slowly to the bottom of the cask, so you take the wine out
through the stopcock leaving the rest on the bottom, then you
clean the cask as thoroughly as possible, and then put the wine
back, leave it a few days, and do it all over again. Now you've
finished the main work. You leave the wine in the cask until, say,
Easter, when you can start to bottle what you need. But there is
one by-product of the harvest you can have earlier than that,
on the day you start making the wine, and that's the early juice,
the must, or *mosta* in Italian.

'But you must keep it in the fridge,' Ornella, Sergio's sister,
instructed us, 'or it will start to ferment,' and as an added
thought, 'we have it for breakfast.'

The equipment in Sergio Contini's garage is among the
most modern you can find, and yet you'll find it in most
storerooms and garages around Umbria. The *botte*, or casks,
are made of translucent plastic and Sergio's hold three hundred
litres each. As he pointed out, you make the necessary calculations as to how much you might need. There's nothing new in
this: in my Loeb edition of Columella, there are pages and
pages of calculations as to how big a field is, how many vines
you plant, and at what distance, how wide the space between
the rows to let the plough through to work the soil. Sergio
Contini has his modern calculations to do but the system is
essentially the same nearly two thousand years after Columella:
Sergio has seven lines of vines a hundred metres long, with
about three metres between the rows to let his tractor made by
Ferruccio Lamborghini, a wine grower too before he died,
keep the earth clear of weeds. Those vines produce nine
hundred kilos of fruit, and generally a wine-maker would
expect about sixty per cent of that to be the finished product.
It's a high return on your investment, unlike olives, where the
return is less than fifteen per cent of the crop.

Once the vines are established they tend to produce well
every year, but need a lot of tending and spraying to keep

disease at bay. There's an old country custom in France where roses are planted at the end of every line in the vineyard, because roses are susceptible to the same diseases as vines but get them first. I did not see this early warning system in use in Umbria. So there's the cost of fertilizer and spray and hard work it is using these cans slung on the back and pumped with one hand while you point the nozzle at the leaves. We do this on our one vine over the pergola and that's more than enough. The spray, not the only chemical now used in wine-making, leaves curious turquoise-like blotches on the leaves.

The actual machinery, the *sgranatrice*, the stripper, has a screw-like implement inside, invented, I think, by Leonardo da Vinci five hundred years before, as a system for pumping water up a hill, now used in all sorts of ways, not least in stripping the fruit from the stem for the wine-maker. That can cost a few hundred pounds, so too the *torchio*, or wine press, which is made of metal with chestnut wood slats, then the casks, with their plastic body and stainless steel fittings and, finally, the big glass bottles with plastic padding round their bellies and big corks in their mouths. Add to that a traditionally shaped oval cask that looks like cement but is lined with glass inside to keep wine for a year or two and I don't think you'd be looking for much change out of £1,000.

I always fondly hoped that we would find more traditional items somewhere: the old bucket-shaped wooden containers which, slung on the back, held the picked fruit until it was emptied into the boxes on the back of the tractor's trailer but no, all those are now in the antique shops, lulling the tourist into thinking that Umbria has not changed since time began. Some wily *contadini* sell up the old wine-making equipment for as good a price as they can get and invest in the more modern productive plant. Wherever you go in early October among the villages around the lake, the same telltale signs of the *vendemmia* are there – the piles of red plastic boxes in which the fruit is put are glimpsed through the open doors and, in the white casks, the wine is gently bubbling as it ferments.

Sergio Contini's wine is light and usually white, with a hint of a bubble in it, and he's very proud of it. Quite right too, I've enjoyed many a bottle alongside Ornella's superb cooking. Mario Pazzaglia, on the other hand, makes a good red wine, also quite light though fruity in taste. I once let Sergio taste it and he grudgingly admitted that it wasn't bad. Leonardo Pascale, the builder, makes a much sharper wine, again a red. All agree that as there are no chemicals involved, you can drink as much as you like and not get a headache the next morning. Though I must say this seems to be theory on their part as I never saw any of them drink in the way the British do. A glass or two, and then the stopper goes back on the bottle. Their grudging admiration for each other's wine, however, is part and parcel of the belief that what you grow and make is the only product you can trust.

Because we don't make our own wine, we trust the wine made by our friends and now hardly ever buy commercial wine, even though Umbrian wines are beginning to be recognized outside the region. The whites of Orvieto are well known, and the late Ferruccio Lamborghini sold up his sports-car business to concentrate in his last years on making local wine on his estate in and around the village of Panicarola. This was a high tech operation, if ever there was one, but what would you expect from a man who was an engineer first and foremost. I never really appreciated his wine. I tried the wines from the co-operative, which produces the Colli del Trasimeno – these are good, solid whites and reds and you can buy them in bulk if you like. They fill up your own cask from what is in fact a petrol pump, which measures the number of litres and reads off the price just as it does at a garage. There's another new wine on the Umbrian scene, well, relatively new. It's the Torgiano winery, a few miles outside Perugia. The owner, whom I have not met, is Dr Giorgio Lungarotti, who produces, say the experts, an impressive Rubesco Red and a white Trebbiano blend called Torre di Giano. I've tried both and liked them.

However, no matter how good these commercial wines, I think I have adopted the local habit of not really trusting these commercial undertakings: why spend a few thousand lire a bottle when you can get good wine for much less? So I have done a deal with Mario Pazzaglia. I can see his vines at the top of the hill, and I watch them grow. I'm sure that is why I buy from him, not the fact that it works out at 6op a litre. Since Mario's last vintage had seemed to me an excellent one, I could not imagine what this year's would taste like, nor could I wait, so I put in an order for a couple of cases before I left.

After all this activity, Victoria and I went home on that second Sunday in October to eat the fruits of our harvest: four magnificent figs, our own tomatoes in a salad with our own basil and, as we looked out over the olive grove, we wondered whether the fifteen trees with fruit would yield us a couple of litres of oil ... Slowly but surely we too were growing and eating our own food though in ridiculously small quantities but our own none the less.

7 The Gastronomes of Umbria

WE ALL SPEND SO MUCH of the daylight in Umbria growing it, or watching it grow, that food – and its preparation – are the inevitable topics of conversation round the table after sunset. It's through talking almost endlessly about food with friends and neighbours that you are given tried and tested family recipes and it's more than likely that each recipe comes with a piece of family history. You can trace the beginnings of many a friendship to the table where a shared appreciation of the culinary possibilities of the aubergine, for example, soon extends into all areas of life and involves births, marriages and deaths. There's some unwritten law which put simply says, 'like me, like my food'. I firmly believe that you will discover more about Umbria, the Umbrians in particular and the Italians in general around the table than through any other form of study. I'm not talking about eating in restaurants or pizzerias but in homes where the barriers come down, the voices are raised and inhibitions disappear. Short of being born an Italian and being raised on an Italian mother's cooking, food is the passport to the Italian soul.

Take a typical evening. We have invited Sergio Contini and his companion Maria Cancedda from Sardinia to supper. Victoria decides to make pasta *à l'amatriciana*. The recipe, as Victoria would tell you, is straightforward enough. You take some *pancetta*, those tiny chunks of smoky bacon, which you buy in the supermarket. You fry them until crisp in olive oil, along with some *peperoncino* (chilli powder), onions, garlic and then add some peeled tomatoes, which you stir gently together until mixed. When the liquid has been reduced a little, you add some finely grated Parmesan cheese. That's the sauce amatriciana style. Obviously you can serve it fresh, but Victoria now freezes it, so that we always have some ready for when we arrive in Umbria on our next trip.

The evening we eat it, we bring it out, cook the pasta (we like the broad, flat tagliatelle), pour on the sauce, mix and serve. That evening we had a few small antipasti: a little mushroom purée on toasted bread, a *bruschetta* and a few slices of a favourite salami of mine called Perugino (like the painter – stocky, spicy and robust). That was eaten without comment. Then the pasta.

Sergio, more than Maria, is just a little apprehensive. After all, Victoria is not his mother, whose cooking he still not only remembers but seems to taste when he talks of it. Nor is it his sister Ornella's, who inherited all his mother's talent and recipes and who, adding a few from her late husband's side of the family, more than holds her own in the kitchen. Nor is it Maria Cancedda's, his companion of many years, whose cooking, he freely admits, is a close rival to his mother's, even though Maria is from Sardinia and therefore has different taste combinations to bring to the kitchen. Indeed, to admit he likes her food, to admit such a fact in public, denotes the closeness of their relationship. 'I love your cooking' is the equivalent of 'I love you'.

Common sense, not forgetting good manners, stops him from any such declaration with regard to Victoria. Yet, a very masculine complication in this part of the world, he cannot insult my choice of partner by insulting her cooking. But Sergio is not just Italian, he's a Roman, and as pernickety as they come. What's worse, Victoria is not Italian, even worse she's English and she's cooking an Italian dish. That's three strikes against her. If this were baseball, she'd be walking.

But Sergio's eaten here before. He now concedes that Victoria can cook, remarkably well for a foreigner he has admitted. But lest hubris take over when she's in the kitchen, he also remembers and likes to recall in a gentle bantering way, the first time he was sitting at the table with us that Victoria's asparagus risotto came out more like rice and asparagus soup than a succulent thick risotto. Also, he likes to recall that the colour of the substance placed before him did not really resemble either risotto or asparagus. He ate it, gingerly, but felt that a friendship based on a lie would never be sustained. So he told her where he thought she had gone wrong. Victoria took it in good part but as a naturally good cook, she is as hurt when something goes wrong for the guest. Over the years this is such a rare occurrence as to render the failed risotto in Umbria unique.

These days Sergio, as all our friends, have watched with admiration and sometimes awe as her grasp of Italian cooking has progressed. Victoria has worked very hard at it, taking notes at every opportunity and, despite my need to watch my weight, using me as a guinea pig for any new dish she wants to try. Sergio knows her ingredients are as fresh as can be. He and his sister Ornella have invested a lot of time and effort in making sure that Victoria cooks as a good Italian woman should. So now, a few years on, he's prepared to enjoy the food, but the need to be seen to be an expert, to be considered a fine judge of matters gastronomic overrides his natural good manners.

What follows is a piece of pure theatre. First Sergio looks at the plate, sizes up the colour, the smell rising slowly, and he savours it. There's a very slight nod of approbation. As the head inclines, the eyes dart in Victoria's direction as if to say, it looks good . . .

Next he picks up his fork, almost gingerly at first and, without waiting to see whether the rest of us are served, dips it in, twirls it and, leaning forward, takes his first mouthful. Victoria, poised over the pasta, with her serving fork in mid-air and about to deposit some on my plate, waits for Sergio's verdict.

Sergio uses the moment to extract all the drama he can. We wait a few seconds more as he scoops the last bit of tagliatelle into his mouth before he delivers his judgement. A Solomon could not do it better.

'*Buonissimo*,' he says to the assembled company around the table, 'very good,' he adds in English so that Victoria can bask in her success. Then, after a few seconds, before Victoria can really relax, he tells us, 'Mind you, it's not a real amatriciana.'

Victoria tells him she followed the recipe.

'Ah, but you need to be in Amatricia to do it properly. Well, that's what they say down there.' Sergio tells us the story of how the mayor of this small town, worried in case other cities might get the credit for one of Italy's great pasta dishes, issued a promulgation that the true amatriciana was made only with smoked streaky *pancetta*, not those mean little lumps that you buy in a supermarket. The pasta was not tagliatelle, which Victoria had used because we like it, but short *penne*, those small little tubes of corrugated pasta. There was, said Sergio, a huge debate about whether onions should be added. In the end the onion won. Not onions as we know them in England, but those sweet Mediterranean onions that add such taste.

'Never use pepper, but *peperoncino*,' said Sergio, the ground-up version of red peppers, which grow in every Italian kitchen garden. 'The pepper you English use is not healthy. It can damage the stomach.'

What was remarkable about this short lecture on just one Italian dish was that, as Maria pointed out, 'What does Sergio know about such things? He has never cooked anything in his life.'

'But I know what I like,' said Sergio, 'and that makes me an expert.'

'Every weekend I do all the cooking, make the sauces and prepare the vegetables, for him to eat if I go down to Rome to look after my business.' (Maria is a dressmaker.)

A few days ago she had made an olive sauce for pasta which Sergio had judged 'excellent'. Maria said, 'All you have to do is put it on the pasta.'

'But it's the way you put it on the pasta,' said Sergio, 'that's what's important.'

'Men,' said Maria, as Italian women always do when their menfolk have made another outrageous claim to be superior, even in the kitchen. But it is true nevertheless that when a man in Italy is happy with the food, the family is happy. Even though in the towns the Americanized fast-food chain is beginning to make inroads into the traditional diet, in the country-side it is still the Italy where the food on the table is fresh and grown within sight of the house and where the annual seasons change the food that is eaten.

'Twas ever thus. Epicurus wrote one of the first cookbooks, or at least a book about food. All those early writers on agriculture I quoted, Varro, Columella, Cato, all worry about the quality of the food that's grown. Pliny talks about food in his letters. But maybe the most persistent worrier about his food was the Merchant of Prato, in always writing to his long-suffering wife, Mona Margeritta, about how to prepare this or that, preserve this food, that fish, or keep this fruit. As printing came into existence, the first real Italian cookbook appeared, written by Platina in the 1470s and called *Il piacere onesto e la buona salute* ('Honest pleasure and good health'). And the great artist, Michelangelo, was not above telling his cook what he wanted for supper. In his case, boiled spinach fried in oil with some garlic and onions. The painter Annibale Carracci has a wonderful picture he called 'the bean eater', the nickname for Florentines, a man in a broad-brimmed hat, a bowl in front of him, some bread at the side.

Victoria, sometimes, used to get just a little peeved by Italian men offering her advice on cooking, when it was the woman who did all the work. I happened across Gillian Riley's translation of Giacomo Castelvetro's advice on fruit and vegetables for the Countess of Bedford in 1614, because he felt that the English diet was too stolid, too meaty and didn't have enough healthy greens in it, salads and the like, not to mention the delicate use of herbs to bring out the taste. Poor old Castelvetro didn't have much effect: a couple of hundred years later, Parson Woodforde, the country vicar, tells in his diary of the years 1758 to 1803 when he spent most of his time eating the very stuff Castelvetro thought was so unhealthy. On New Year's Day 1790, he had some skate and oyster sauce, pea soup, ham, chicken, a boiled leg of mutton and capers, a roast turkey, fried rabbit, brawn, tarts, mince pies etc. All washed down with a few bottles of claret. I get the impression that most Italians still think we British eat in this fashion, and which is why so many of us die young of heart attacks.

But the two races have always been able to feel superior to each other when it comes to commenting on each other's eating habits. Early travellers to Italy did not find the food much to their taste, nor the inns for that matter. Tobias Smollett in the eighteenth century was always scathing while in this century, D.H. Lawrence was never complimentary about the food he found in the country – usually a thin soup with some scraps of meat in it, which had been boiled and boiled.

An English woman, however, changed once and for all the British view of Mediterranean food. Elizabeth David, when most Britons had never tasted olive oil let alone seen an olive, wrote her first book on Mediterranean cooking in 1950. That was barely a generation ago yet now the received wisdom in all parts of the western world is that the Mediterranean diet is the best and the most healthy, and modern-day Italians most certainly think so. Hence the popularity of Italian restaurants in Britain and America but the food one eats in even the best of them never quite has the taste that you find in Italy in the most surprising places.

In Castiglione del Lago there's a restaurant called La Cantina, whose speciality is pizza. My favourite is with truffles. Never have I had a truffle-tasting pizza in Britain or anywhere else. And in La Cantina they are cooked by a big, round lady in a white overall, rather like a doctor's, with a little white hat on her head. All evening she stands in front of the two large ovens, where the wood burns white, and the pizza are shovelled in and out with a long-handled wooden spade and, within minutes, taken straight to your table.

It was for a combination of all of the above reasons that we set out to learn as much as we could about Italian cooking. I say 'we' but, in reality, it is Victoria who has borne the brunt of the research. But before feminist readers cry 'stereotyping', let me add that Victoria has always seen cooking more as an art form than a chore. Italy provided her with a huge canvas. What's more, it was a common-sense move too, for we had started to grow some of our own vegetables, the shops usually stocked what was seasonal, but most of all friends and neighbours tended to give us as much of their surplus produce as they could, so the fridge and the vegetable store were always full to overflowing. Giovanni Filipini, I recall, arrived one summer's day, with an extremely long yellow vegetable, which he called 'Sicilian *zucchini*', freshly picked, which we all ate for lunch in a *peperonata* (cooked red, green and yellow peppers, with a bit of fresh *pecorino*, sheep's-milk cheese, just grilled quickly on the top). We had enough for lunch, and the leftovers were served cold as a starter next day at supper.

Maybe it's age, or just the subliminal messages about eating less meat that are such a part of modern diet sheets, but we seem to have moved, in Italy at least, to a more vegetarian diet and only notice how little meat we eat when someone serves us a little lean tender veal, or some chicken baked with rosemary. Ornella can surprise us still with a little something that turns out to be made with meat, like some minced young lamb in herbs, served in small round shapes the size of chicken eggs.

The question we now ask ourselves is whether there is such a thing as real Italian cooking. The quest has turned out to be as elusive as that for the Holy Grail. There's a style and some common traditions, allied to a range of basic ingredients that everyone uses – tomatoes, garlic, oil and herbs like basil, parsley, rosemary and sage. Tomatoes are the most ubiquitous of plants, yet it's odd to think that they are of only comparatively recent origin in Italy, the Romans, for example, had never heard of them.

Everyone we talked to has their own way of preparing everything, which they maintain is the best way. Only a couple of books, published in England, have given us really good guidance. Foremost is Antonio Carluccio's modest but marvellous tome, *An Invitation to Italian Cooking*. He too likes to tell you where he ate the dish and with whom before passing on the recipe. The other book is Beth Romer's *The Tuscan Year*, which lovingly offers the cooking of her neighbours. Once again, it's place and people, as much as ingredients, that are important.

In our case, the person who has played a central role is Sergio's sister, Ornella. She has been the great teacher, sometimes seeing Victoria, I think, as the daughter she might have had. Every time we go to her house for supper, she turns out some new dish for us to try and to tell us how it is made.

One of the most memorable meals was one New Year's Eve when we had the traditional sausage and lentils. They say in Italy that you must eat lentils because if you eat a lot on New Year's Eve, you will earn a lot of money. Sometimes it's the names that are unforgettable as much as the food. There's *pasta alla chitarra*, for example, which is pasta but the dough is actually laid on a guitar-like contraption which cuts it into the long, thin strips for cooking. Ornella says the idea is from the Abruzzi area but I've seen these contraptions in many places now I know what they are.

The Italian pizza is a very different dish when cooked at home. None of the really thick pie crusts so beloved of the American-style pizza houses in Britain. Ornella's pizza is as thin as can be, but crusty like a biscuit when you bite it. And the toppings are kept simple, just a smear of the homemade tomato sauce, a few mushrooms, maybe a bit of sausage *e basta*, nothing else. I think it'll be some time before either of us plucks up enough courage to use our own bread oven, having spent one memorable evening at Ornella's when she cooked pizza for us in her wood-burning oven.

There are certain rules. The wood, maybe chestnut or

maybe oak, is cut into small strips and bound together. They are called *fasces*, the symbols of the old fascist state, but here there is no political significance. These burn more easily and it's when the oven looks white inside and there's virtually no smoke, that you slide in your pizza on the great wooden shovel. In a very few minutes, so thin is the crust and so light the topping, that it's cooked and ready to eat.

Now here's the clever bit. You make one pizza per person, so for six people six pizzas, but the trick is to come up with six different ones and when the first one comes out, you give about a sixth to each person, the same with the next one and the next, until each guest has had a whole pizza but six different tastes. The wood does give the pastry base a special taste I must say, recalling for me the days of long ago in front of the fire in my home in Wolverhampton when I was very young and we toasted bread, then buttered it, and ate it straightaway. Central heating may be more comfortable but it makes lousy toast.

In Umbria, and in most places in the country, you will see these outside bread ovens. Now they've started producing designer ovens that don't have the same charm for a foreigner like me, but that keep alive the tradition of cooking outside. I say 'bread oven' but that's not really accurate. Often you will see meat being roasted in such ovens. I suppose you could argue that the Italians invented the barbecue. The basic rule in Italy is, whatever you cook, indoors or outside, it must be brought straight to the table.

The second rule, in the country at least, is that as far as possible you should know where all the ingredients have come from. Better still if you have produced them yourselves, failing that at least you should know who grew them. I remember the *bruschetta* with Giovanni and Elizabeth Filipini. Elizabeth makes the bread, Giovanni grows the garlic and makes the oil from his own olives. The chestnut wood is from a tree on his land. Only the matches and newspapers for the fire come from outside.

Victoria finds that to prepare a proper meal she is largely kept away from the table unless she works hard with the starters or antipasti, which can be eaten cold or tepid and don't need to be be cooked there and then to get the genuine flavour of the dish. But now that all our friends know of our interest in cooking, when Victoria goes to the kitchen to cook, say the pasta, everyone goes with her. Sometimes she has a little too much advice and shoos us all out again. But you can't be an Italian and not have an opinion about the way something is cooked and which you are prepared to defend to the death.

The shape of the Italian meal becomes obvious too as you become used to the way it progresses from the antipasti, the small tasters before the pasta course. Then comes the *primo*, or first dish, usually of fish, then *secondo*, which is usually meat. Then come the sweets, or *dolci*. The problem in restaurants is that foreigners like us don't always eat right through the set pieces. I take an antipasto and Victoria has a small pasta starter. Too often for comfort we've forgotten to tell the waiter that we want both dishes together, so I get served first, and Victoria has to wait until I've finished and my plate is taken away before she gets her pasta. Once I waited and waited before starting my antipasto, which of course meant that Victoria never got served. By and large we stick as most Italians do now to one main dish, reserving the grand banquets for special occasions, such as the sixtieth birthday party we attended in a swish hotel in Montepulciano, where there were ten courses. Luckily each was a tiny one, so the overall effect was not too bad on the stomach and its digestive abilities.

That is the joy of Italian food. Most Italians are very figure conscious, whatever their age, and the consequence is that they eat relatively little even if there are a large number of dishes. Rarely does one take a second helping, even though masses of food will have been prepared. The Italians are cock-a-hoop that their cuisine is now reckoned to be the healthiest in the world and, like anyone who is considered a success, they have relaunched a massive amount of interest in cooking and diet in the country. It also means that you can ask anyone for the recipe and they will give it to you. Which brings me back to our culinary mentor-in-chief, Ornella.

Somehow she seems to hear of our arrival almost before we've got the bags out of the hired car and into the house. The phone rings.

'It's Ornella, when do you want to come over for supper?' That's always the first question before she asks about our health, the journey, or even the weather in England. This last question, I have to say, is one that all Italians tend to ask, as if the knowledge that it might be cold or raining only reinforces their firm belief that to be born Italian and live under a Mediterranean sky is a gift straight from God. And who are we, pale-skinned creatures from far beyond the Alps, to gain-say such a belief as we push south in increasing numbers every year in search of the sweet life?

Even though every time we are determined to resist her hospitality for as long as we can, she insists and it is almost invariably that within twenty-four hours of arriving at the house, we make the drive down the hill, through the village, and then half-way along the road that leads to Castiglione. We turn off near the rather unfortunate local cement works and then drive, bumping along an unmade road, to Ornella's house hidden among the trees. The huge iron gate is open ready for our arrival. Now we arrive on time, seven-thirty on the dot. We used to leave a little leeway, believing it impolite to be there on the stroke of half past seven. But we've learned that good manners in Italy demand a prompt arrival. The front door opens, almost as soon as we ring the bell, and there stands Ornella, a woman of a certain age, but in the Sophia Loren mould, tall, well made, handsome . . . and dressed to the nines even for a simple evening with friends.

Ornella and her late husband bought the house many years ago, as their small place in the country. When he died seven or so years ago, Ornella left Rome where they lived and set up home on a more permanent basis. Her brother Sergio, now retired and separated from his wife, moved in with her at first to look after the land: the vines alone produce a few hundred litres of white and red, all made in the huge shed behind the property beneath a small apartment. It was because of this small apartment, which we once rented while waiting for our house to be made habitable, that we met brother and sister.

The short let was arranged by a friend of Giancarlo Caponeri's and in many ways I think Ornella and Sergio did it more as a favour to the friend than from any need to earn money. The first time we met them was on the morning after moving in for a week's stay. Sergio knocked at the door of the *villetta* as it's called, and shyly offered us some home-made apricot jam, and a small fruit tart freshly cooked in Ornella's oven that very morning. These were the first of many gifts from Ornella's kitchen, each with that special taste of food that is cooked *con amore*.

In those days we spoke very little Italian, and while Sergio can speak a little English, and Ornella a little French, conversation was mainly over the table, with murmurings of approval at the food we had been given. Nowadays we have more vocabulary and there's a five-year friendship between us all, including a visit by Sergio and Ornella to our house in London. The conversation has developed, but so too has the range of tastes and sights that have greeted us on so many evenings.

Yet the evenings also tend to follow a certain ritual, no matter how many people this amazingly gregarious woman has invited. First we have 'un drink', maybe a little vermouth, or a little whisky. Then we move to the table while Ornella goes to the kitchen from which she emerges a few minutes later with the first course displayed on plates on a small trolley. Then comes the main surprise – hare cooked in wine, a huge risotto, a massive pasta with some delicate sauce. The conversation ebbs and flows but at some point Ornella will explain how she cooked the sauce or the pasta or the hare and Victoria takes notes, while I sneak another small helping just to make sure that I have correctly savoured the dish in question.

Mostly the food at Ornella's is accompanied by Sergio's homegrown wines, the light very slightly sparkling white, or the delicate reds. His proud boast is that there are no chemicals in the wine, nothing that will keep it for years. All of the wines, therefore, are but a few months old. They are light yet fruity and go perfectly with the vegetables and fruit, all of which comes from the *orto*, or cottage garden, which is watered every day by a DIY irrigation system of a plastic hosepipe leading from the well near the apricot tree.

Ornella loves company, and so some evenings the house is full: her brother-in-law Giorgio Polumeni and his wife Mirella, both from Rome and her sister-in-law Nora, who lives in Messina in Sicily. And various nieces and grand-nieces and nephews. Great swirling evenings of laughter and food, and a little wine . . . but in the end we are all drunk on each other's company. Each of them has added something to our culinary knowledge. Sometimes you come across marvellous country recipes that seem to take an age to prepare, like Maria Cancedda's country soup with fourteen ingredients.

'Name them,' I said and she did.

'There are carrots, potatoes, peas, asparagus, mushrooms,

fennel, three sorts of beans, spinach, artichoke, plus rosemary, basil, and garlic. And you can add *peperoncino* too if you like, that would make it fifteen ingredients.'

As I soon discovered, a plateful of that for lunch on a brisk autumn day and you don't need to eat again for hours.

Equally there are dishes that we've gathered from restaurants where we have eaten and where the waiter or the owner is only too happy to share the recipe with you. Eating in some of these places is a surprise. There's no menu but the owner comes up and tells you what he is cooking that night. Maybe it's only one or two dishes but, if you can't decide, he says you can have some of each, rather than a good helping of just one.

One of the most remarkable experiences to be had is in a place near Lake Montepulciano. I went there unexpectedly with Giancarlo, Leonardo, his wife Nila, and the rest of the team working on the house, with their wives as well. It was a dark, cold, late October evening, not long after the restoration had been started. I was in Italy to do a programme for British Forces Broadcasting about Afsouth, which is what the Naples-based NATO headquarters on the southern flank of the Treaty Organization is called. Organized by the Americans, who always make media trips work, I had all my interviews, up to and including the four-star admiral in charge, over and in the can two days earlier than I expected.

I had a rental car and the trip from Naples, past Rome and up to the Chiusi exit is motorway all the way. So it was only a handful of hours at most to go to see how the house was progressing. In fact, it was almost finished. I recall only the radiators had still to be installed and some of the electrical wiring. I stayed as usual at the Miralago Hotel in the centre of Castiglione. It is not a place to try and remain incognito and within the hour I had a message from Giancarlo inviting me out, as he put it, for a surprise dinner party with the team. I asked him when we met whose birthday it was. Nobody's, he said, the surprise was the place where we were eating. It was a misty night and, as Giancarlo drove me along the narrow lanes and over bumpy tracks, I completely lost all sense of direction. Suddenly we stopped in front of a row of rather battered looking old houses and knocked at a front door. An old lady opened the door and without a word let us into the main room. It had a couple of light bulbs hanging from the ceiling, both at least one hundred watts so with the white walls and the white plastic table covers, the place almost made you whatever the electric-light-bulb equivalent of snow-blind is. The trestle tables had been pushed together to form a long single table set diagonally across the room.

The rest of the party arrived all together within minutes. Nazereno, the plumber, the life and soul of the party as always; Fabio, the electrician, quiet but always smiling; while Leonardo quietly took charge, telling each man where to sit and placing each man's wife as far away from her husband as possible. Sergio Sargentini, the surveyor, came too, the only man with a tie on and there were one or two others I did not recognize. I suppose we were twenty in all.

'What's on the menu?' I asked Giancarlo.

'Wait and see, is that what you say in English? Wait and see . . .'

We did not wait long for, after a glass of wine and a quick nibble at the rough country bread which was in plastic boxes strategically placed along the length of the table, suddenly the old lady reappeared, holding open a door which led on to the kitchen. Out came an equally old man, her husband, carrying a massive iron pot. This was my first introduction to what the people in this part of Umbria like to claim as their best local dish – *tegamaccio* – a stew made from fresh-caught fish from Lake Trasimeno, including of course, the fish they call *La Regina*, the queen, carp.

The smell was magnificent, fishy yes, but controlled by the herbs that had been added. The dish was put in the centre of the table and, as we passed up our plates, the old man on one side and his wife on the other ladled out the portions. Even after twenty dishes had been filled almost to overflowing, there was enough for at least another twenty helpings, maybe even more.

I didn't get the recipe that night. These were early days when the whole venture was so new, it was more the problem of getting the house finished that preoccupied us, not what food we would eat once we moved in. It was a mistake. On one or two occasions Leonardo has offered to take us back there but each time it has been shut. The old couple only seem to work when they feel like it or when the ingredients are to hand. The place is their home and, though the fame of their *tegamaccio* is known far and wide, like most Italians they work more when it pleases them rather than others. This is their little part of the black, unofficial economy and so they call the shots. I've tasted the dish in other places, even in La Cantina in Castiglione where the pizzas are the main attraction, but it was a pale imitation. I cannot tell you how robust, I think that is the word to use, how robust was the combined taste of great chunks of bread in the base, the thickish liquid, the herbs and vegetables but most of all the various types of fish.

I've not found a recipe for *tegamaccio*, I'm not even sure how it's spelt. But the word *tegamatu* in the dictionary means 'panful' so it might be a dialect equivalent with the *di pesce* ('of fish') being taken for granted. The usually comprehensive Antonio Carluccio gives a recipe for fish soups which he says, unhelpfully from my point of view, can be found in every seaside town or fishing village. He doesn't mention lakes. There is a less than 'robust' version of it on the menu at the

Miralago Hotel but I have not bothered to ask for their recipe since it does not taste like the old couple's unforgettable creation, which I consumed with such delight that October night in the front room of their house near Lake Montepulciano.

Another restaurant near a lake, where the food is interesting is La Fattoria, on the edge of Lake Chiusi. It's an old farm-house, covered with Virginia creeper, set in its own grounds, part of which is set aside for campers, in the main French or German. I don't recall ever seeing a British family spending a couple of weeks under canvas there. There are two dishes that I make a beeline for – the first is a starter of tomato, mixed with what we are told is stale bread chunks that have been soaked in water, a little lettuce, cucumber chunks cut small, some onion, and basil mixed with an oil and balsamic vinegar dressing. Whether I would have eaten it knowing it was stale bread, I am not sure but the efforts we have made at home to reproduce the dish all taste of, well, stale bread.

Victoria's Yorkshire determination not to be defeated by what seems on the face of it a simple concoction takes us on an occasional pilgrimage back to La Fattoria to taste the real thing. It's called *panzanella* and it is frustrating that everyone else seems to get it right and we can't. The Fattoria is also good, as far as I am concerned, for whole squid roasted on a spit and rubbed with a little oil but that's a very personal taste.

You also get a good *panzanella* at another local restaurant called the Bistecara, in a small village called Panicarola, the home town of a very famous Italian, Ferruccio Lamborghini, whose automobile and subsequent agricultural machinery busi-nesses made him a very rich man. The locals, jealous or some such, never seemed to be that pleased that he had made so much money or that he came back to his home village. No-where, not even in the Bistecara, could you find his wines, either red or white. Somehow, you felt, the local people thought it took more than just a lot of money to make good wine. When Signore Lamborghini died at a good age in the summer of 1993, there was a long obituary in *The Times* of London. I didn't find a mention of his passing, though, in the *Corriere dell'Umbria*. Perhaps they felt that driving his farm equipment was enough of a monument in his own region.

The Bistecara restaurant has a special attraction for us in the huge range of antipasti on display and to which you help yourself – different sorts of mushroom, zucchini, egg plant, fennel, all sorts of beans, broad beans, french beans, and tomatoes, roast and stuffed, *bruschette*, green olives, black olives ... we have never managed another course since we discovered the place. But the attraction has to be the display as much as the taste. The huge variety makes you believe that you could taste one dish a week and still not have tried them all.

All this may be just a part of living in Umbria, the green heart of Italy, as they like to call it in the tourist brochures but when you see so much growing around you, and every meal no matter how humble or simple has so much taste, you do become a little obsessed with the food. Oddly, you eat less but better. I have lost weight here. But why let me try to persuade you with words, when you can try some of the more simple recipes for yourself? I have picked at random just half a dozen given to us by friends and neighbours and, in the case of the first one, by a waiter in a restaurant in Perugia.

The centre of Perugia, a vast brooding city set on hills like Rome, has a long history stretching back to the Etruscans, traces of whose building you can still see in the thick walls that surround parts of the old city centre. It was a Roman stronghold, then fought the pope, became part of the Church's dominions in central Italy but, whichever side Perugia was on, it had as bloody a history as any of the city states of Italy. They try to avoid eating salt in Perugia because they were forced to pay a salt tax to the Vatican once.

Off the Corso Vannucci are lots of tiny alleyways which, as the late, great travel writer H.V. Morton remarked in his book, *A Traveller in Italy*, really make you feel what it must have been like to wander the labyrinths that were medieval cities. It was down one of these alleyways that we went in search of lunch one hot summer's day.

Through a small door, down some stairs and you are in what are the cellars of the building. In front of you, a huge counter with a glass front, in reality it's a cold cabinet of the type you find in supermarkets and there on display was an enormous range of dishes, starters, main courses and sweets. We asked for a dish of antipasto and left it to the waiter to choose for us. We had some red peppers, aubergines and carrots. We told the waiter how good his choice had been, especially the carrots, which we had not had before done in such a way.

'Oh it's easy,' said Franco, 'my mother does them for me . . .' and he gave us the recipe:

Boil some carrots, not to destruction in the British way, but *al dente* in the Italian manner, and cut them into sticks. Meanwhile fry a little garlic in extra virgin olive oil and add the carrots. As they cook, add some *peperoncino* and finally a little vinegar. It's best not to eat them that day but leave them to marinate for a day at least, serve them cold as a starter and you have a delicious mixture of sweet carrots, with a spicy tang from the *peperoncino*, and just a hint of garlic to finish it off.

Frittatas are another simple dish. Essentially they are a mixture of potato, or other vegetables, fried in oil and served turned out of the pan and sliced rather like a cake. The most basic we came across was Ornella's potato *frittata* on one of her favourite events, the picnic. This one was quite an adventure because it involved a trip across Lake Trasimeno to one of its three islands. Two of the islands are still inhabited, Isola Maggiore and Isola Minore. The third is called Polvese and was once owned by a salami manufacturer, I think, but is now owned by the town council of Castiglione del Lago.

You get there by a small steamer from any of the little fishing villages around the shores of the lake, and you arrive on the island at a rather grand *embarcadero* which looks vaguely Chinese in design. There's a caretaker and his family who live on the island but otherwise it is now deserted. The big house remains and there are the ruins of a church and a Franciscan monastery at its highest point, and a small beach area, where most day trippers stay. Ornella, using the men as pack mules, led us out along the edge of the island towards a narrow tip. Here we were alone, diving off the rocks, sunbathing on a small patch of sand and when the time came, picnicking in a very serious manner.

We had a range of cold snacks and thin cuts of hams and *carpaccio* beef. But it was the *frittata* that I remember most fondly. Once again it's the simplicity that appeals, and the possible variations. But the problem is that, like all good cooks, Ornella knows instinctively how much of each ingredient you need, so be warned, you need to taste as you go.

Take two chopped onions, two tomatoes, parboiled and skinned, half a glass of white wine and mashed potatoes. You fry the onions lightly in the olive oil, add the tomatoes, some salt and *peperoncino* and cook until the mixture becomes dryish. Then you add the wine and cook, again on a high heat until it's dryish. At that moment you put in the mashed potato. Mix together and pack it all into the pan and fry until browned.

You then turn it out on to a plate, so that the browned portion beneath is now on top. Served warm, it's a tasty way to serve potatoes with anything.

You can't go far in Umbria without having a pasta dish. The local version of spaghetti is called *picci* and is slightly thicker than is usual in Britain. Once again, it's local pride demanding a local dish. Maria Pazzaglia is always passing on the benefit of simple sauces for pasta. This particular one involves peas, which I had not come across in a pasta dish before. (We add peas, however, to mushroom risotto both for colour and the slightly sweeter taste it gives the dish.)

I leave you to cook the pasta as you see fit. But this is Maria's sauce:

The ingredients are olive oil, a chopped onion, a bunch of parsley, two tomatoes, peas and salt and pepper (or *peperoncino*, which I prefer whenever possible). You fry the chopped onion, add the chopped parsley, the skinned tomatoes, mashed up, and the peas. You cook the lot over a high heat for up to ten minutes but be careful not to burn. You pour the sauce over the pasta and serve with just a sprinkling of freshly grated Parmesan cheese.

In theory, Parmesan should come from Padua, says Sergio the food critic, but you can also use mature *pecorino*, the sheep's milk cheese. The secret of a good pasta sauce is that it must not, as my son and daughter John and Natasha think, completely cover the spaghetti, but be rather served sparingly so that the taste of the pasta and the sauce intermingle.

Another pasta dish comes from Pepe Mancuso, the carpenter from Città della Pieve. Before I tell you about Pepe's dish, I must introduce the man himself, because every day we are in Italy we think of him. Pepe, a Sicilian by birth, was trained in London as a carpenter, before marrying his Spanish wife and moving to Città della Pieve where he has a small shop, selling restored antique furniture, and a wonderfully mysterious workshop up a side street in this little town. The workshop is full of bric-à-brac and old furniture; rising from the sawdust and clutter some wonderful pieces emerge. Pepe, bearded, intense and a true artist, was introduced to us by Giancarlo as someone who might want to restore a wooden cask used by grape pickers at harvest time. Today such baskets are all plastic but these handmade tubs were once slung on the back and filled with grapes. We found this old one on a dump and, sure enough, when Pepe had finished with it, it had a lustre that that must have been there the very first day it was made, and never since.

It was while Pepe was handing this over to us in his workshop that we spied an old bedhead, a Louis Philippe style called *letto barco*, or boat-shaped. We admired it, and Pepe said, 'If you like, I'll make you one.'

It took a year but now stands in all its massive glory – a bespoke bed, six foot six by six foot six, both ends with that slightly S-shaped look, made in chestnut. It is our pride and joy and the reason why, whenever we are in Italy, not a day passes when we don't think of Pepe and thank heaven for the day we found an old tub used by grape pickers many years ago.

We also remember Pepe for a family recipe for penne, baked in the oven with aubergines. Again it's so simple:

You need some oil, a pound or so of skinned tomatoes, fourteen or so basil leaves, penne and some Parmesan cheese. You slice some aubergines and fry them in oil. In a pan you put some olive oil, reduce the chopped tomatoes, add salt and pepper, and basil leaves. When you've cooked the penne – al dente – you put some of the tomato sauce in the bottom of an oven dish, then some aubergine, then some penne, then some aubergine, layer on layer if you've lots, finishing with some of the sauce, and then sprinkle some grated cheese on the top. Pop it in the oven for up to twenty minutes. Hot or cold, it's a mouth-watering combination of tastes.

A similar recipe, but without the pasta, was given us by our neighbour, Giovanni Filipini. The length of his house on the southern side is covered with vines, both fruit-growing and ornamental, which give the most marvellous shade in the summer. And we had gone there one morning to taste a little of his wine and some of his tangy radishes, served with little chunks of ripe mature *pecorino*. Inevitably we talked of food and the huge amount of produce that his *orto* gives him every year, more than enough for his own needs, and more than enough for him to be exceedingly generous to neighbours who aren't there long enough to grow all their own vegetables. For this dish, as we left, he gave us everything but the cheese. By now I'm sure you can guess some of the ingredients: oil, garlic, tomatoes, onions and courgettes. (But, he says, you can use any of the plants in the family, as well as aubergine.)

You fry a large sliced onion in oil, with garlic, thinly sliced courgettes and tomatoes (skinned and parboiled so that they mash easily). Cook till the vegetables are softish, add seasoning, salt and chilli powder, then sprinkle a little mozzarella cheese on top and pop under the grill. Again, this a dish you can serve warm or cold.

This last dish came to us because one evening we were having supper with Sergio Contini and Maria Cancedda and I mentioned that a pheasant had adopted our house, rather as robin redbreasts do in Britain (we have two in North Kensington who come back every year). Most mornings when I'm in Italy early in the year, I catch sight of a pheasant wandering across the grass, hopping up on to a wall and then disappearing off into the olive grove as if on a morning constitutional. I assume it's the same bird but, as I'm not an expert twitcher, you have to take my word for it.

But my joy as a city dweller in sharing the beauty of nature was lost on Sergio who told me I should catch and eat it, because pheasants are a noble dish. Maria had a marvellous recipe which uses all the herbs in the Italian garden:

> This dish involves thyme, origano, tarragon, rosemary, juniper berries, fennel, chopped carrot, celery, garlic and onion, all put in red wine in which you marinate the pheasant, cut up into pieces. You leave this overnight. The next day you take out the meat and fry it in olive oil until it's brown and tender. Reduce the sauce in a pan and pour it over the meat and serve with salad.

I think our pheasant got to hear of the recipe because he – or was it she – disappeared a few days later and I haven't seen the bird since. When Sergio asked me if I'd tried the recipe, I told him that the main ingredient had gone missing. With a promptness that was breathtaking, Sergio said, 'We have some pheasant here, come and taste it.' It was a superb dish. The next day our own pheasant made its reappearance, obviously scenting that the immediate danger was past.

A final thought, just in case you are wondering, given all the jokes about my weight on the *Today* programme. The Mediterranean diet does work, I don't put on weight. No longer would John Timpson, were he still on the programme, be able to quip, as he once did after reading a flash from the travel unit that a huge load was holding up traffic on the M1, 'Ah, young Hobday must be going somewhere.' I am, John, to Italy.

8 Ourselves and Other Animals

YOU CAN NEVER have a place in Umbria entirely to yourself. You have to share it, whether you like it or not, with the animals and insects that abound in the area. There's nothing new in this of course. You could say that we are continuing the traditions of Umbria in that in the past the ground floor of these farmhouses was always used by the animals. We still have the remains of one place where horses or donkeys were kept and which we now use as a store for garden equipment.

It's the one room on the ground floor we will never do up because it reminds us so much of how the house looked when we first saw it half a decade ago – the old beams, the walls without plaster, the tethering post, troughs along the walls, plus wooden bars at the window and an old wooden door on its rusted hinges that just about manages to survive each winter but which we coat lovingly with modern wood preservative every spring. Now much of that has disappeared even in those houses which have not been done up and in which the original owners, the locals, still live. With the plough drawn by oxen replaced by tractors and the mules to pull the small carts replaced by the three-wheeled truck, the ground floor is more of a garage than a stall. Ours has become a dining-room and a kitchen but, even though we've replaced many of the old doors with newer ones that keep out the draughts of winter, we still have to reckon with the fact that the house is crawling, and I mean crawling, with animals of one sort or another.

When the warm weather comes, for example, the wasps buzz up to the walls, looking for tiny cracks in the rendering between the bricks, so that they can find a warm spot to spend the night after sunset. In the last remaining room, yet to be restored, a large square space in the centre of the house at ground level, it's almost impossible to go in, so many wasps have made their nests. But even in more frequented spaces, such as the gas *bombola*, under the plastic covering over the dials which give you the fuel level and so on, I once had to run for my life because I had disturbed a nest. It took a jet of water from a hosepipe to remove the small, mushroom-shaped honeycomb from the plastic casing, even though it only seemed to be attached with a substance about the thickness of a pin. Every year we get another surprise and find yet another species is sharing our Italian home. We may call it Casa del Lauro but in reality it should have been named Casa Animale, Animal House.

We no longer take anything for granted once we are inside the house either and we open the cupboards and drawers in the kitchen with extra care ever since we disturbed two snakes slumbering one sultry August Sunday. They had wrapped themselves around a bewildering assortment of string, candles, a pair of scissors, an empty oil can and all the other essential household paraphenalia usually shoved out of sight in places which are rarely visited. At first we did not realize what we had found. We thought it was the tail of a largish lizard and expected it to scamper off as soon as we made to touch it. As we moved things, the tail got longer and longer. Almost shyly it revealed itself, uncurling its body which it had woven into something like a ball of thick, dark-coloured wool. The snake – there was now no mistaking what it was – seemed to have woken up from a deep sleep, it moved so tentatively, even cautiously. Then, all of a sudden, it slithered away and once again curled itself into a tight ball, this time looking more like a Gordian knot of bluish-green rope. I didn't need a tape measure to tell me it must have been at least a metre in length.

I'm a persistent coward when it comes to snakes so it was Victoria who pulled out the whole drawer as quickly as possible to empty the contents, snake and all, on to the floor. But, as she did so, suddenly a second snake slithered out of another part of the drawer and hid itself in the cupboard below as its companion sped across the terracotta tiles, a greenish-blackish blur against the dull earthy-red of the floor. My manhood in question, I rooted about in the cupboard with a suitably long piece of wood until the second snake made a dash for the door and they both disappeared across the tufa terrace into the grass and out of sight, leaving behind a pile of things on the floor of the kitchen, an upturned drawer and two very startled human beings.

Oddly it was in what is now the kitchen that the builders had found a huge snake when they had started to clear away the old rather smelly stalls to lay the floor in the first place. They beat it to death, not hesitating to explain that it could have been a viper. 'Better safe than sorry,' said Leonardo, the builder from Calabria where it is said to be wiser to strike first and ask questions afterwards. Leonardo, the most gentle of builders but who is afraid of no man, is right to be scared of vipers. They can kill. Indeed so dangerous are they that catching one merits a paragraph and your picture in the local paper the *Corriere dell'Umbria*. Only two days after our encounter, the paper ran a story about four boys who went fishing in the small lake of San Mariano, where they saw a viper asleep under a rock and stoned it to death. Experts from the nearby town confirmed it was indeed a viper and the article ended with a warning that vipers are dangerous.

It was a couple of months later that I saw my first dead viper, wedged between the forks of a stick and carried triumphantly by a chap from the next village, who had been out walking with his dogs near the house. When I asked him what it was, he said proudly that it was a viper and, shooing the dogs away who came to sniff and possibly eat the dead snake, he showed me its ugly head which he had battered with the flat side of a small cleaving tool he was carrying with him, for what purpose I didn't like to ask. 'It's deadly, and very dangerous,' he said. 'A dog could die if it ate it now it was dead.' I'm not sure how true that is but I did take a careful look at the snake so as to be able to recognize it. It was not as long as the two we had found, maybe a couple of feet at most, probably about eighteen inches in reality. Down the dark green body there were black marks, little jagged shapes, like those slashed sleeves you see in films about the Borgias or the Medici on television. What was worrying was that he had found it at the top of our hill, under our favourite shade pine, where we like to stand in the evening to watch the sun go down over Chiusi. We take a stick with us now to that spot, keeping one eye on the ground beneath us and only paying half the attention we should to those magnificent summer sunsets that fill the sky with a marvellous deep orange colour as the sun slips quickly behind one of the mountains over towards Siena.

To the best of our knowledge, the snakes we found were the rather more friendly grass snakes but it'll be a long time before I forget the fangs spitting out in anger as they moved away. Or the limp dead head of the viper hanging from the stick but still looking as if it wanted to fight back.

Yet, such is the advantage of time passing, that four years on, I now entertain the fanciful notion that the snakes we shooed away from the kitchen were descendants of the snake Leonardo the builder had killed. They had returned instinctively to the place of their birth, now a shrine to their ancestor. It's a very Italian thing to do, and why should Umbrian snakes be any different? The Italians call it *campanilismo*, that all-encompassing word that ever so loosely translated means that a person firmly believes in the perfection of the village where they were born and that no other place can possibly compete for their affections. And also the place where they would want to be buried. Strictly speaking, the word *campanilismo* refers to the bell tower, the *campanile* in the village church, so I suppose you could call it the bell-tower fixation . . .

The biggest and best known saint in Umbria, of course, is St Francis of nearby Assisi, in many respects the first 'green' politician in history, who believed in the power of nature as God's work and that animals, His creations, were due as much respect as humankind. So is it any wonder that here of all places, in the centre of the Italian pensinsula, animals of all sorts would feel at home? As he wandered the woods that still cover a great part of the land surface here, St Francis must have got to know a lot of snakes as well as all the other animals he used to preach to and bless. We are farther from God in the twentieth century and so too at a greater distance from the animals and other creatures that we have come across and learned to share the house with; some we cursed to hell, others made an accommodation with and others came to love.

We realize now that we shouldn't have been surprised by anything we found in the house or outside it. Here in Umbria there is more space, and land is going spare, so wildlife of all sorts can prosper. Here it is man that is the intruder in their domain, not the reverse, as in countries like England where the old forests are in retreat and motorways are forced through ancient meadowlands. Here, in our part of Italy, when it comes to animals, reptiles and other creatures, we have enough types to start our own zoo.

Not all the native species are friendly by any means. My particular bugbear, so to speak, is the mosquito. At first we were fearful, constantly wiping or spraying exposed bits of flesh with an odd-smelling product called Autan. Sunset was the danger time, because that's when the mosquitoes come out to play. We sprayed and fumigated, set traps, and generally moaned every time an insect landed on us or our plates. Yet, after a time, all this wild life has a rather calming effect and much to our surprise made us feel more at home, rather than being visitors. In London one sees the occasional fly, a dog on a leash, or a cat purring in a friend's house, or traces of pigeons on the car in the morning after these annoying birds have rested in the branches of the tree above your parking spot. In Umbria animals abound and you'd better get used to them.

But don't run away with the idea that we've become clones of St Francis and welcome everything that flies or walks into our patch. Some we have declared war on. Among the pests, the mice and the ants are the most persistent, followed by the mosquitoes and a whole range of other flying, stinging noisy little beasts. It's a constant but losing battle to try to eradicate them. Our confidence took a knock when we picked up a leaflet in the town hall. The leaflet was from the *servizio di disifestazione* which was run at the local level by a national organization rejoicing in the very Italian name of 'Pest Control Italiana', based in Forli.

The leaflet gave us some useful but alarming intelligence about the enemy. In Italy, it said under a beautifully drawn mosquito climbing a single blade of grass, 'In Italy, there are sixty different species of mosquito; it takes eight days for the eggs to hatch, and the female needs a meal of blood (*pasto di sangue*) to go to the full term of its pregnancy.' If that wasn't bad enough, on the facing page was information about the *chironomide*. You might well wonder what that is. My large Sansoni English/Italian-Italian/English dictionary couldn't tell even though it claims to have over 240,000 references and 570,000 translations. There are four hundred species of these little pests and they lay their eggs on even the smallest drop of water. They don't bite, thank heaven, but they are the things that crowd round lights in vast numbers at night and swarm into the house if you leave a door or window open without any kind of netting to keep them out. Pest control says, turn down lights or, better still, put a bright light at the bottom of your land to attract the moths and the rest away from the house.

Whatever you do, you can't escape all these things, so you declare war. As always, defence expenditure tends to outstrip disposable income if you are not careful. First of all, the enemy is blessed with overwhelming numbers and if one species doesn't get you, then hundreds of others will. You start, in the early days, with the simple spray can: there's the rather impressively decorated Baygon, from Bayer in Germany. Its principal enemy is either the mosquito or the fly but down one side are some exquisite little drawings in black of up to ten varieties. There they are, one under the other, just as the RAF during the Second World War used to paint a swastika on the fuselage of their aircraft to denote how many of the enemy had been shot down. The two main varieties on the front of the can are all in black too, up to twenty, maybe thirty, times the size in real life, each with six legs and see-through wings. Baygon promises 'quick action and long-term potency'. But spray too enthusiastically and you too are driven from the room you want to clear of mosquitoes.

Very quickly you start to scan the shelves in the household goods section at the local supermarket. Now you want the power of death without the smell of the chemical. That's when you discover VAPE in all its forms.

First of all, we used the famous VAPE mat treatment, known to all travellers in the hot climate of the Mediterranean summer. Again, like research into weaponry, the VAPE people have been developing new and deadlier weapons to kill the mosquitoes. There used to be a stick of greenish solid stuff that you lit and let burn slowly. The smoke was supposed to kill off all the flying insects and, if it didn't kill them, its odour was sufficiently repellent to keep them away. It does work in the garden but after a time the smell gets to humans as well, or at least this human. Next comes the VAPE mat. This is a marvellous little gadget that consists of a small dish-like object, into which you place a tiny, rectangular green (that colour again) tablet. You plug the dish into the mains and the heating of the dish releases the tablet's fumes. The humans don't smell it at all and they do seem to work very well in the house, especially the bedroom. But now VAPE have come up with VAPE Magic, the ultimate weapon in mosquito control, possibly even the final solution. According to the leaflet, you can plug in the VAPE Magic and, even with the lights on and three windows open, no insect will even come into the room.

I was intrigued to discover that the product was made under licence from a firm in Japan, which rejoices in the name of

Fumakilla. Without Japanese knowhow Italy and its foreign residents like us might still be bitten to death over the long hot summer by a variety of flying insects. And the plague, which used to ravage this part of Italy, carried by the lice and flies of that era and which killed thousands including my hero, the painter Perugino in an outbreak in 1523, might still be controlling humans, rather than humans controlling insects.

It's not so long ago since Lake Trasimeno and much of the surrounding area was a malarial swamp. One wonders how they lived even in the cities without any of our modern protection against these flying and at times kamikaze-like little pests.

According to some very unscientific research conducted among local people, I have managed to find some of the natural remedies that they used to keep the mosquitoes at bay and to minimize the effects of bee stings and the rest. And the first remedy is there for everyone to see when they drive or walk around rural Umbria ... the omnipresent geranium. This, it appears, has an odour on its fur-like leaves that no mosquito and some other flying fiends can stand. That's why the geranium is seen on nearly all window sills, even wedged behind the iron bars that have been put there to keep out human invaders. As Maria Pazzaglia said when she told us about the geranium, 'Not just a beautiful flower but useful too.' I tried rubbing the leaf and smelling the stuff that sticks to the finger. It would keep me away from any house that smelled like that, let alone a small mosquito going about what he believes to be his lawful business of sucking the blood from human beings to give to his ever-pregnant wife.

The next remedy is used if the geraniums have failed to deter. This time the odour is quite acceptable but some people in England might wonder what you had been up to if they caught a whiff on top of a number seven bus. If you want to keep the mosquitoes away, take the dark green leaf of the herb basil and rub it on the exposed skin. If you prefer another odour, then wild mint works in the same way, although you might feel rather like oven-ready spring lamb. If a persistent bug still manages to get you, try rubbing a basil leaf on the bite; it immediately calms it. I know, I have tried it, though I smelt rather like an Italian salad. Yet another ready remedy, against bees this one, is to rub garlic on the bite. This seems at odds with an old medieval trick: I was told by Sergio Contini that people up to no good in the alleys of cities like Florence or Perugia often rubbed garlic on the blade of a dagger which, it was said, meant that a wound would never heal. That I have not tried on myself or anyone else.

The basil cure for bites I can recommend. There is another plant that works well, too, so I am told. They say that the tomato plant leaf provides an antidote to stings. I haven't tried it yet, but one day if the little buggers don't give up, I'll cover myself in geraniums, basil leaves and tomatoes and defy them to do their worst. Maybe, though, I'll forget the tomatoes. Mine are small enough without me pinching leaves every time I get bitten.

The ultimate deterrent, I'm told, in the southern half of Italy but alas not in Umbria as it is not hot enough, is the house lizard the Sicilians call gecko. They eat mosquitoes. Which is why, even though most Italians aren't very caring about animals in general, they will never kill a gecko or a lizard.

Happily, animals, plants or chemicals are only part of the armoury against the silent enemy that bites in the night. There are now gauze nets you can have installed in the windows to keep out unwanted nocturnal visitors. They are quite expensive, very efficient, but have one main drawback. They are so finely made that they keep out not only the insects, but almost any hint of a breeze on a very hot night. So you sweat unbitten and hardly sleep even though you are safe.

The one anti-mosquito device we have not installed, because Victoria absolutely refuses to even think about having one, is a gadget which electrocutes the mosquitoes who are attracted to it. Mr Galiotti has one hanging in a rather splendid oak tree. It looks like an electric fire and it emits a bluish light. It seems the mosquitoes cannot resist the light or the odour and fly, like airborne lemmings, towards it. What puts Victoria off the idea is that the death of each insect involves a sizzling sound as it is electrocuted on the machine. At the height of the mosquito season, it's like having a small fish and chip shop above your head, so constant is the sizzling sound.

But while we can wage our own war more or less successfully against the mosquitoes and other flying insects, mice are a very different proposition. Here, I believe, you have to get professional help. Mice seem to make their homes somewhere in the house, in the walls or under the floors. You never actually see them, though. You find a few droppings in a corner. You turn the bed and find a small hole chewed in the mattress. The corner of a cushion has provided some small rodent with a square meal. You know they are there, lurking sight unseen until you shut up the house and go away, and then the mice come out to play, nibbling as the mood takes them, on a patch of material just in the middle of that nice new T-shirt.

It was through the mice that we met the rat catcher of Chiusi, Dottore Giovanni Bonomi. The *dottore* in his title was meant to reassure. This was no ordinary slayer of vermin. He had a degree, he was an expert. We could have every confidence in his abilities. We could also expect higher prices. The *dottore* was very tall for an Italian, I'd guess at least six feet four, his height being such that he had developed a slight stoop, which went with his rather lugubrious nature. His face was like that wonderful character actor in British films in the forties and fifties, Alastair Sim. Dottore Bonomi smiled less. He grimaced rather. But then, if you went around killing rats and mice all day, you too would be rather lugubrious. We found him in the Yellow Pages and he turned up in a big Landrover, laden with equipment, chemicals and so on. He was a little like a medical doctor in his approach with a 'what seems to be the problem' opener to the conversation. His voice was deep and his speech slow. For once we could understand every word. The problem, quite simply, we told him was that we seemed to be overrun with mice. They had chewed the bottom of the sofas, left droppings all over the place and eaten their way through a woollen blanket on the bed.

Dottore Bonomi asked our leave to inspect the house and could he do it alone? Off he went for what seemed like an hour and told us that indeed we did have a lot of mice and that he would try his best to get rid of them but we had to realize that, in the country, leaving the door ajar for a second, even the narrowest gap, and the mice would rush in. He then rooted around in his Land Rover, painted bright green, because he was a man who kept the environment healthy, and pulled out some yellow plastic boxes with holes at one end. These he placed strategically in every room in the house and then put inside some things which looked like sweets in purple wrappers. On no account were we to touch these sweets. They were very toxic but the mice could not resist them.

Our concern was that we would be left with the carcases of dead mice all over the place. At this suggestion, Dottore Bonomi allowed himself a self-indulgent smirk at our innocence of the cleverness of this particular pest-control system.

'What happens,' he explained in his doleful voice but this time with just a hint of excitement in it as he revealed the tricks of his profession, 'What happens is that the mice eat the poison and then crave water and rush out of the house into the fields, where they swell up and finally burst, leaving no mess at all.' Victoria, with an almost St Francis-like love of all animals, wanted to stop the treatment there and then. I told her to think of other things, like a clean house and no mice droppings every time we came out from England. I think housewifely pride finally overcame animal rights. Dottore Bonomi made two more house calls. Like a true doctor, he adjusted the dose since the patient was not responding to treatment. He made some technical changes in the deployment of the bait, shifted the yellow plastic containers a centimetre here, half a centimetre there and we seem to have been mouse-free ever since. But doors are still very quickly shut and all house guests instructed to keep them shut to keep out the hordes of marauding, blanket-chewing, sofa-eating country mice. And, to this day, we have never found a single body.

I wish I could say the same for ants. Ants are of another magnitude . . . Here we are dealing with millions and they are everywhere. Once again it's chemicals, once again a spray can in lurid colours, green and yellow, which acts fast it claims, not only on ants, but cockroaches as well. I sometimes wonder whether it's all the same stuff, with only a label change, rather like badge engineering, as it is called in the motor industry, where only the radiator panel and the shape of the wings are altered, but everything else is pretty well standard. Once again market research has shown that as long as you paint, in black, larger than life images of ants or roaches, it will sell. I can't say that I have carried out a complete survey of everything that comes in cans to kill insects, flies and so on, but, on a limited sample in my local supermarket near Castiglione del Lago, most of it is of foreign origin, which makes me think that maybe the Italians have built up a tolerance to attack which we foreigners cannot match. Most evenings, as I drive up the hill past Luigi the water diviner and his neighbours, they are sitting out on the steps talking away ninety to the dozen, as do the locals in other small villages, all seemingly oblivious to the threat and presumably tolerating the discomfort when attacked.

But to come back to ants, it seems no matter how much you spray, or how much powder you put down, the ants keep coming. Like trench warfare in the First World War, they charge the enemy on a broad front. In the end you can only study them and, like Robert the Bruce, who learned a thing or two about spiders (yes, we have them too), as you watch them scurry here and there, carrying bits of grass, or bits of twig, huge loads many times their own weight, you can only admire their tenacity. If you've a cruel streak, and sometimes it will overcome you, try washing away an ant home; it'll stop them in their tracks for only as long as you hose the spot. But when you stop, they go back to work and next day pretty well all traces of your flood attack will have been eliminated. Like so many animals here, you can just about keep them under control. Cover all food, keep the kitchen and eating areas as clean as possible, and sweep up any crumbs as soon as they are dropped. But defeat the ants, never.

But not all the animals here are enemies. The most fascinating, even though they have made their homes in every nook and cranny they can find, are the lizards. These are not to be confused with the gecko. Umbrian lizards eat something but I have not yet been able to find out what, but heaven knows there's enough flying food in this part of the world to keep even the most discriminating of creatures happy.

Lizards can stand quite still if they see you and if you don't move, you can stare at each other for as long as the mood takes you. But give the slightest twitch and they shoot out of sight. They can walk up vertical walls, and even across ceilings, presumably with some kind of suction device on the five fingers on their four feet. What's quite amazing is that they never seem to suffer from concussion no matter how far they drop. They can startle you sitting under the pergola when, in the height of summer, the leaves of the vine provide most cover, there is suddenly a frantic rustling then, plop, down comes a lizard on your head, bounces off and then hits the ground . . . and when I say 'bounce' I mean bounce. As soon as they hit the ground, they are scampering away to the shade or some tiny hole in the wall where they've made a home for themselves and their families.

Sergio Contini, a man with an unlimited supply of facts about almost everything, told me that when lizards mate, the male holds the female by the tail. When she is finished with him, she breaks away, leaving her tail behind . . . hence so many tail-less creatures in spring when they first emerge from their hiding places.

Now from the sublime to the slightly ridiculous – the wild boar. These, as I explained earlier, are a favourite quarry for the hunting groups in the area. You don't often see them, however, by day when they hide from human beings in some deep part of the wood, in the shade and are usually asleep. One night when we were driving home, about eleven o'clock, a huge boar, I think female because it was followed by three very small animals, scurried in front of the headlights. Early one morning, I saw a young boar moving down in the little gully below the house but it was gone before I had a chance to get the binoculars to be sure. What you do find though, after a wet night, are the footprints of a family, and small areas of ground where they seem to have scuffed the earth looking for food. If I had really taken my tracking badge seriously as a boy scout all those years ago, I could easily follow them to their lair.

Pheasant abound, strutting their proud way along the edge

of the fields, and quite often strolling, there really is no other word for it, strolling through the olive grove. There's rabbit, of course, which Mario quite often traps for the pot. In fact, what with the wild pig, the hares and rabbits, the pheasant, not to mention the occasional pigeon, I don't really understand why the Umbrians of old are said to have had such a basic and largely meat-free diet. A dedicated hunter should have been able to feed his family quite well.

The oddest find one day was a frog underneath the spreading juniper on the edge of the terrace. Now this tree is the variety of fir that spreads out at low level, so it looks rather like a fir tree that has been sat upon by an elephant. Perhaps, when Hannibal got his last elephant down to Trasimeno in 217 BC, the Punic hero turned the animal loose and, as it rested after the long trek from Spain and across the Alps, it sat on local varieties of fir thus creating the species. But that's by the by, our juniper has been home to a frog one summer. There are frogs in the Mancinis' water hole across the way but it's still quite a hike from there to our tree . . . there's no water on the way and a lot of open ground to cover. I thought frogs needed cover and damp to survive. Obviously not all of them do, because this frog stayed in the shade all day. It was after watering the garden one evening that Victoria saw it move. From then on, generous and kindly woman that she is, she watered the juniper every day, giving the frog an extra helping of water. She says she read Toad of Toad Hall when she was young and can't help herself. The result was that the tree spread even farther, until Giulio, not knowing that it was home to a frog, cut back the branches hard the following spring and we've never seen the frog since.

In the end, it might simply have been that the call of its friends and relatives across the way became irresistible, and it took the long hike back to its home pond, like all Italians preferring life in its home village to anywhere else in the world, no matter how generous the owner is with the water supply.

Another animal we've been told about is the porcupine but it only made its presence felt after I cut myself badly on that day on the terrace and bled rather profusely. When I got back home after my trip to hospital, the blood on the stones had disappeared and the cracks between the stones had been dug out. As Giulio said laconically:

'I didn't know porcupines liked human blood.'

Let's end this visit to the Umbrian animal kingdom with the sad story of a dog that came to die. One morning while we were having breakfast under the pergola, we noticed a dog, a hunting dog, very lean and spare, lurking near the tomato plants, round the corner from the gas container.

At first it just stood there, with its head hanging down, looking lost and hungry. Victoria's heart went out to it immediately and she got some water, despite my rather old-fashioned notion that all foreign dogs may have rabies. It refused the water and just stood there looking at us reproachfully. It hardly moved. The sun got hotter, and the day wore on and the dog hardly moved. By lunchtime it was lying down, in roughly the same spot where we had first seen it. Over lunch, it again refused any water, just lying with its eyes gazing at us, seeming to ask us to help. By two in the afternoon, this is five hours after it had suddenly appeared, it started to shiver a bit and then first one leg and then another would judder and jerk. That was when we could not stand the sight any longer. What else does a British couple do in a foreign land when confronted with a suffering dog, but call the police.

Within minutes a small Fiat with two smartly dressed *carabinieri* arrived. We explained the story but, by this time, the dog was obviously in agony and having convulsions.

The police radioed for a vet and one arrived about ten to fifteen minutes later. A large, jovial man with glasses jumped out of his rather larger Fiat with a little black bag . . . again, we patiently went through the story.

'It's poison,' he said, 'I don't think it'll live much longer.'

The death throes, for that is what we had been watching nearly all day, now reached a climax as the dog lying on its side went into an almost constant convulsion, each leg shooting out here and there, trying to raise its head as if to get up. The four of us, the two *carabinieri*, the vet, Victoria and I, watched until the shuddering stopped and the animal died.

The vet, wearing plastic gloves pronounced the death official and we put the dog into the hole we had dug for the grass cuttings, covered it over, and then heard the vet speaking confidentially to the two policemen.

'Listen lads,' he said in hardly more than a whisper, 'report this and there will be a lot of unnecessary work for us all.' The phrase he used in Italian was *una grande confusione* and he tapped the side of his nose with the index finger of his right hand in that knowing way of the world-weary official.

'Let's say nothing,' and he turned to me, '*d'accordo?*' he asked me.

'Agreed,' I said.

After the perfunctory handshake, they all left. The vet would not accept anything for his time, the police saluted. Sworn to secrecy, we did not tell anyone except Giulio, who said it was either a piece of poisoned meat put out to trap a fox or a viper, which takes us back almost to where we started.

9 The Mystery of Pliny's Villa

BUT WHAT ELSE DO YOU DO? ask friends and colleagues.

'After the house and the land, and collecting recipes, and tracking down Peruginos, what else do you do?'

It's a hard question to answer without sounding like a culture vulture. Like so many ex-patriots, whether part time like us, or full time, like so many who have gone before, and will follow us, much of the appeal of Italy is the historical contribution, those amazing periods when it was the centre of power and the arbiter of civilization. Someone once wrote, and I've tried hard to locate the quote, that around ninety per cent of the world's acknowledged art treasures are still to be found in Italy *in situ*, still looking more or less as the artist intended them to look when they were created.

Only the Italians seem blasé about all this heritage. The rest of the world seems to worry more about it and, as when

Florence was flooded, it seems that foreigners are keener to dig deep to save the city than the proud Florentines themselves. And Venice, too, that serene city on the water, is worried about more by foreigners like John Julius Norwich than say, Silvio Berlusconi media magnate and now politician. Of course I think that a lot of this apparent lack of interest is Italian make-believe. For once, they don't have to praise what they do, here they really can leave it to others. And how sweet it must be when a portly foreigner like me talks enthusiastically about the latest art treasure he has seen. What's more, all Italians know that their world has survived flood, famine and foreign invasion, not to mention domestic politics by the bucketful, and that they will survive whatever happens in the future.

So I'll stop making any more excuses. We love the place and rejoice at our good fortune in spending so much time here. We are hungry to know more and see more. So when we come across another place we'd like to see because someone mentions it in a book, we say, 'Well, while we are here, why don't we . . .' and off we go, bumping down the hill, into the mad traffic of the *autostrada* until we find the exit and plunge once again into a countryside that seems to have been untouched by progress of any sort.

Sometimes we are disappointed, the tourist trade has got there first, so if anyone is fool enough to visit Assisi in high summer, then he will instantly regret the effort. The same goes for Florence or Siena in the summer. But the part-time ex-patriot can miss all that. We spent nearly a whole day in the Uffizi in Florence in January with only five other people for company. We wandered the *campo* in Siena on a freezing New Year's Day but, while blowing on our fingers to get the blood back to the tips, we could appreciate more than most what an amazing architectural creation that space really is.

And when we heard about the hot springs of Bagno Vignoni where five hundred years ago Lorenzo, the most magnificent of the Medici, used to bathe to try to cure the gout that finally killed him, we went there one frosty December morning, and swam in the salty waters looking out over a deep valley, past an arrogant ruin of a castle on another slope towards a snow-capped Monte Amiata. To add a touch of mystery to the view, we gazed on it through the steam that rose from the warm water like a light morning mist in early spring. And we had the place to ourselves.

In August or July we stay at home in Umbria but, in May or June, if we've a mind then it's off to Urbino over what they call the Mountains of the Moon, to stand alone in the Palace of the Duke, savouring the beauty of the place. Most of the ideas for day trips come from the books I've been collecting. It's a deep philosophical question, did the books become necessary because we built in so much shelfspace to the house, or did we put the shelves there because we knew that sooner or later they would be filled with books? I've read so many books on Italy now, chasing this or that historic personality or fact that I'm beginning to understand not just our debt to the Italians for art and music but also for the philosophy that is the basis of so much modern thought. And it all means more when you are in the country: like those heroes and villains from the past, you take a break from the pressures of the world to tend your vines and worry more about an April frost killing off the tiny and so vulnerable greeny-white shoots on the olives. Much better that, than spending brain power on whether a Conservative prime minister can survive a drubbing in the local elections, or whether the Labour Party has done enough to win the people's trust the next time there's a general election.

The whole point of a place in the country in this part of the world is to escape and to think of other things, like Boccaccio, who set his *Decameron* in a villa where young men tell each other stories to while away the days. It was the Italians who perfected the art of creating a rural haven to which they could retreat from time to time to refresh their spirits and tend their bodies. Horace, the poet, wrote nearly 2,000 years ago: 'This was among my prayers: a piece of land not so very large, where a garden should be and a spring of ever-flowing water near the house, and a bit of woodland as well as these.'

If Horace came to my place in Italy today, he'd see that I have the answer to his prayers. And that's what makes me, I suppose, just a little self-satisfied with what we've achieved, despite the advice of one friend who said knowingly five or more years ago: 'You are very brave, I wouldn't attempt such a thing ever. Think what could go wrong!'

Well, brave or no, we did it. And now we have more time to savour the achievement. Unlike the annual holidaymakers, we are out in Italy as often as time permits, or a cheap flight is available. We've spent time in the house over the years, in each of the twelve months of the calendar year. We've seen it under snow, we've enjoyed spring and autumn, we've sat outside on lovely and surprisingly warm December days. We've walked in the gales of January and sunbathed at Easter. And while we leave, with regret every time, we know, with luck, it's only a matter of weeks before we are back.

In some ways perhaps that's why we feel we have done the right thing. There was a television documentary on BBC, which looked at the experience of a number of couples who had sold up and moved to France, to open an hotel in one case, to run a vineyard in another. They all deeply regretted the move, and all had money worries.

In our case, by trying to combine two lives, by keeping what earning power we have in one country, while spending what we made in another, we get the best of both worlds. The hard work in the one is more than compensated by the relative peace and quiet of life in the other. And it's a very special quality of life, which brings me back to my original point of departure. Here in Italy we have a very real sense of space and time. While making plans for the future – a new pine tree here, yet another laurel there, maybe courgettes will be planted this year, not peas – we also find we share the interests of so many of our predecessors in this part of the world, those who have been privileged to spend part of their lives in the foothills of the Apennines.

The timelessness of such an existence makes even the most historically distant man or woman seem like a near neighbour. Like Machiavelli, who was exiled to his farm when he found himself in the wrong place in the labyrinth of Florentine politics, I can spend a day outdoors and then, after sunset, change and shower and take down a book from the over-crowded shelves and travel back to some other age. Let me quote Horace again: he said he preferred people to travel so that they could change their minds, not just change the climate.

Which is just another excuse to buy a book. The book buying has worried Victoria because I have such an addiction to books that I cannot enter a bookshop without buying something. Whereas she invests her spare cash in what she calls the 'garden fund', mine goes on books. There's almost a race now between us as to who will have the most in number: Victoria with her laurel bushes, a young one costing the same price as a paperback, or my books which now fill the shelves in North Kensington and all the shelfspace we have in Umbria. I try as far as possible to control it. I've even attempted what drug addicts call the 'cold turkey' cure. This involves going into a bookshop without any cash . . . but then I see something, and out comes the credit card.

Umbria at least has given me some sense of purpose. Instead of buying at random, all the books are bought, so I claim, as research for our life in Italy. It has also meant that Foyle's in London's Tottenham Court Road has become an extension to Italy, especially its classic and arts sections, neighbouring gold mines on the second floor.

It's impossible to pinpoint which comes first now, the book or what has prompted it. Sometimes I visit a place and want to read up about it. Sometimes I'm reading something and conceive the idea that I must visit the actual spot. Most times I don't really care which; because either way I am led along a new path to a new place. A lot of my reading has been chasing down references to the most famous former inhabitant in the Valley of the Fireflies, Pietro Perugino. Sometimes I feel like Casaubon in *Middlemarch*, researching and researching but not yet daring to commit to paper when it comes to Perugino. Sometimes the events just seem to emerge by accident, and lead to yet another little trip to the past.

For example, we almost bought a house near Città di Castello, about sixty or so miles further north from where we are now near Lake Trasimeno. Città di Castello lies in the upper valley of the Tiber, in the most northern tip of Umbria. On her first house hunting expedition, Victoria quite liked the place, a tallish house, she told me, built on three floors into the side of a hill, with a huge piece of land attached and a tobacco tower. But it was too remote, too deep in the country, to be easily accessible. But even more important, from her point of view, the local town, Città di Castello, was too gloomy a place to attract her. Had we bought it I might well have been working on the life of Pliny the Younger, rather than Perugino the painter.

I came across Pliny the Younger by accident when I was researching the ways of the Roman gardeners in Foyle's. I first heard of him when I read the introduction to the marvellous book by Georgina Masson on *Italian Gardens*. She quoted a little of his loving description of his house in Tuscany. But since he wrote that in the first century after the birth of Christ, history has changed the borders a few times and now the house would have been in Umbria, so that made him part of the world I wanted to get to know. And from the first reading of his letters I was hooked. Chatty, to the point and, even in translation, you can hear the friendly voice of this Roman of equestrian rank, a lawyer, and the man whose many jobs included the management of the sewage system for Imperial Rome. He has been confused with his uncle, Pliny the Elder, whose death the nephew witnessed when Vesuvius buried Pompeii. Pliny the Elder had written the first great encyclopedia, a compendium of facts and, it must be said, fantasies and fallacies, about the ancient world, on everything from forecasting the weather to planting trees, cutting gem stones and curing aches and pains.

It was the translation of Pliny the Elder's great work in the 1470s in Florence that helped to establish the classical base of the Renaissance in art, literature and politics. So famous was the elder Pliny that the younger was ignored at best and confused with his uncle at worst. But some scholars knew and respected him, and modern historians have used his letters as a key part of research into Imperial Rome in the first century. But let the letters speak for themselves. Just read this . . . it could be modern Umbria and a summer's day in the twentieth century:

Picture to yourself a vast amphitheatre such as could only be the work of nature; the great spreading plain is ringed round by mountains, the summits crowned by ancient woods of tall trees, where there is a good deal of mixed hunting to be had. Down the mountain slopes are timber woods interspersed with small hills of soil so rich that there is scarcely a rocky outcrop to be found; these hills are fully as fertile as the plain and yield as rich a harvest, though it ripens later in the season. Below them the vineyards spreading down every slope, weave their uniform pattern far and wide, their lower limit bordered by a plantation of trees. Then come the meadows and cornfields . . . my house is on the lower slopes of a hill but commands as good a view as if it were higher up, for the ground rises so gradually that the slope is imperceptible, and you find yourself at the top without noticing the climb . . .

This paragraph comes from one of the longest letters in the whole collection and is only matched by another which describes how he spends his days in summer at his house in what Pliny calls Tusculum, but as I said, now is firmly part of Umbria. I had made a mental note that some day I would like to visit Pliny's villa and see that natural amphitheatre for myself. And my appetite was whetted again when I was reading H.V. Morton's book *A Traveller in Italy*. Like so much of my background reading, I was on the flight from Heathrow to Pisa or Rome, two hours roughly, not counting the delays on the ground or stacked over London because of air traffic control. It is a wonderful way to get over the boredom of modern air travel. Morton was on Lake Como when he got the idea of visiting Pliny's villa nearby, because Pliny talks of a spring which rises for six hours and then falls for another six. He goes to the spot, asks directions and drinks the water from the spring, quoting Pliny extensively as he does so. As Morton wrote:

As I drank my cup of spring water, I noticed a trout rod leaning against the side of the house near the balustrade. I walked over and saw fish in great numbers, some of them two pounds in weight, nosing the water of the spring as it fell into the lake; and I remembered Pliny's remark that in his villa in Como he could fish from his bed as if he were in a boat . . . Under the spell of such continuity I felt that Pliny himself might appear, weary from Rome, tired of pleading before the Centumviri, a court he considered noisy, vulgar, and fallen from ancient austerity, and anxious only to forget the ceremonial toga and put on a country tunic and tell his troubles to Calpurnia.

Como was too far to go from my house, and was too far out of my region to interest me, but Tifernum Tiberina, as Città di Castello was called in those far-off days, was but an hour or so's drive from my village. I can't help wondering as I cover the distances in modern Italy, how much the Romans or the princes and dukes of the Renaissance might have achieved if they could have taken the metalled road in a fast car.

There is a pressing need for the Englishman to make sense of the Italy of today in relation to the Italy that was. It was the main inspiration of the Grand Tour, with men like Boswell suddenly speaking Latin when they reached the Coliseum in Rome. D.H. Lawrence, in his oddly titled book *Twilight in Italy*, is full of the glorious past, the names, the inspiration, as he stays in a cheap pensione on Lake Garda with Frieda. Even Lawrence, Bert the miner's son can't help waxing lyrical: 'In the autumn the little rosy cyclamens blossom in the shade of this west side of the lake. They are very cold and fragrant and their scent seems to belong to Greece. They are the real flowers of the past. They seem to be blossoming in the landscape of Phaedra and Helen. They bend down, they brood like little chill fires. They are little living myths that I cannot understand.'

I read and I reread whatever I could to get to the soul of Italy. It was unstructured, scattered reading. If I saw a book, I bought it for the plane, or for the cool nights when the house was shut up tight against the winds of winter, and watching television would be a sacrilege (how would you feel watching a game show in Italy where bosomy housewives take off articles of clothing every time they fail to answer a question from the leering MC?). Which was how I came across yet another book, *Palladio's Villas*, or life in the Renaissance countryside, by Paul Holberton and it was here that I realized that my humble farmhouse was in the same tradition, though on much more meagre lines, as Pliny's villa or the Palladian masterpieces that have been let go to rack and ruin in this country. But what *is* a Palladian villa?

Holberton explained that the Renaissance élite used their villas as places to escape from the cares of government and that the gardens were as much a part of the whole as the buildings. Indeed, he writes, 'Villa is an impossibly corrupt term. To the English it sounds too much like "Chalet" or villa as in "Holiday Villa".' But Holberton goes further and looks for the roots of the real meaning of 'villa'. 'English and Italian "villa" derives after all from the same Latin as French *viull*. As for the etymology of the Latin word *villa*, it is probably a corruption of the word *vicula* which is the diminutive of *vicus*, meaning both a street and a hamlet, either in the country or the town . . . In classical usage it had come to mean an estate in the country in particular.' Now these estates were self-supporting, with farms, outhouses, quarters for the servants, or slaves in Pliny's day. Pliny has a curious offhand remark about how the climate in Tusculum was healthy, his people much healthier there than elsewhere and he 'has lost fewer of them', 'lose' being a euphemism for 'death'. Which is why so many Romans still escape to the country when they can afford to, to grow their vines and their olives and live from their vegetable garden.

Giovanni Filipini had a bad bout of stones and went on a strict diet. When I asked him what it consisted of, he told me, 'Everything that I grow for myself, and nothing else. So please don't ask me over for a meal this year, I can't eat outside the home.' Little I suspect did Giovanni, a cultured man, realize he was echoing the great Renaissance treatise by Alberti, *Della Famiglia* which, loosely translated, means 'On the Household', the forerunner of Mrs Beeton. Alberti said much the same. Home-grown food is best.

Which brings me back to my hunt for Pliny's villa in Tifernum. You can go over the hills from Castiglione del Lago if you want a winding country route through the sort of landscape Pliny would have known. Hills, trees and a few streams still managing to survive the summer drought. Pliny himself, in winter and spring, would have come up from Rome on the Tiber by small, flat-bottomed boat ... quite a journey since the river winds so much. But the modern Città di Castello was then guarding the head of the river and was an important centre in the days of the Emperor Trajan, with whom Pliny had an extended correspondence when he was sorting out the problems in one of the provinces in modern-day north-west Turkey, then called Bythnia. Just to digress, there was a rebellious sect called Christians active at the time and Pliny sought the guidance of his emperor. He had the habit of asking members of the sect if they were Christian, warning them that they would be executed if they said yes. If, after he had put the question three times, with the warning, they still praised Jesus, off they went to their deaths. Pliny had the habit of sparing those who denied they were Christians, even though he suspected that they were not telling the truth: if they made a sacrifice to the Roman gods, their lives were spared. Trajan agreed that this was a sensible course ... better people pretended to worship Roman gods in public and denounced their religion for all to see.

Given this sort of job on behalf of the Empire, it's easy to understand why Pliny so coveted the time he spent in Tifernum and his other villas or estates around the country, fishing from his bed near Como, or sleeping late at his house near Laurentinum, not far from Rome. In the letters it seems certain that the place I was making for, Tifernum, was by far, far his favourite. As he wrote to his friend, Domitius Apollinarus, 'I enjoy the best of health, both mental and physical, for I keep my mind in training with work, and my body with hunting. May the gods continue to make this the pride of the place and a joy to me.'

The drive north from Perugia takes you up the wide valley of the upper Tiber, there's some light industry just beyond Perugia but soon it's more open countryside, with vines and olives on either side of the road and, beyond the foothills of the Apennines – 'the healthiest mountains in Italy' as Pliny assured Domitius, who was worried that the air in Tuscany might not be healthy. It's not the busiest road in Italy by any means, not half as crowded as the *autostrada del sole*, which links Rome with Florence and on up to Milan. Just beyond the exit for Città di Castello, there's the turn off for Selci Lama and the road to what the map calls the Slopes of Pliny, Colle Plinio . . . the sides of those hills which formed the natural amphitheatre that Pliny described so lovingly. You drive along a narrow road through urban sprawl, the village of Lama having a rather nondescript centre to it. There's a sharp turn to the left which we missed the first time, but which has the name Via del Plinio Il Giovane, and suddenly you are out into open countryside. But there are no signs, nothing to indicate where the villa or its traces might be. We drove up the road, which went past a huge set of walls round an imposing villa. Whatever it was to whomsoever owned it, it was not a Roman villa. Farther and farther we ventured, past a small clump of houses until we felt we had gone too far.

Then, in the middle of nowhere, we saw a bar sign. The end of the house jutted into the road at right angles, the entrance being down a small slope. Under some trees, and beneath the cover of a huge vine, were a couple of stone tables and benches for people to eat out. The doors were firmly shut, but the shutters were just ajar to let in what little breeze there was. Victoria waited in the car while I went to ask the way. As I peeped through a crack in the shutters at the entrance to the bar, a woman's voice from up above called down saying that she would be but a second.

A few minutes later, after some clattering and squeaking of locks, the door was opened and a lady, smartly dressed, full make up, probably around fifty but still with a good figure and with her dyed blonde hair in place, asked me in. It was blessedly cool in the empty bar which looked as if it did not have very much business. It was dark, and only the morning sun shafting through the open door provided the light as I hesitantly asked her where I might find Pliny's villa.

Looking back, she must have thought it the strangest request from a foreigner but she considered the question with good grace. She replied rapidly and with a local accent that I found hard to follow. I asked her to speak a little more slowly adding, redundantly, that I was English. Illogically, therefore, she asked if I spoke French. And she began to explain in such heavily accented French that it still sounded like Italian, that there had been some archaeological work done, back past the big *palazzo*, to the right and right again. I repeated the directions, in both French and Italian. I held out my hand to thank her, and she took it and said, 'If there is anything else you need, please come back.' As I left I heard the locks turning again as the doors were closed once more on the outside world. There was, I felt, the beginnings of a novel here. Who was this lonely woman, who spoke French, took immense care of herself, but lived alone, as far as I could see, with only locks for safety, not even a dog to bark a warning to strangers coming to the place. She was wearing, I remember, Diorissimo.

I turned the car round and drove back towards the villa, telling Victoria of this strange encounter. Past the villa we drove, turned right and then right again and started a long climb . . . there was nothing that looked remotely like a villa from Pliny's day, no signs, no tourist symbols. Just a chalk road that twisted higher and higher up the increasingly steep side of the hill. The views, as they were in Pliny's day, were marvellous. These must have been the woods where Pliny would have hunted to keep his body in trim as he told his friend in the letters. 'Mixed hunting' he calls it. So it might have been wild boar, rabbits, pheasants, who knows . . . But the slopes and the thickness of the trees would have more than exercised him and no doubt made him yearn for one of his cool rooms, where a healthy servant would have oiled him and rubbed him down after his efforts. He would think over a speech, or draft in his mind a letter or two which he would then dictate to one of his servants, while he went on to another subject, or met friends who had come to call, or he would just sleep in the shade and listen to the waters in his fountains, splashing as they dropped back into the marble dish below. All of this and more besides, Pliny told his friends, was what he loved about his summers in Tifernum.

But we were getting nowhere – not even the slightest trace of a Roman villa, let alone a shady room where we could relax after the exertions. But looking back at that flat plain below, ringed by the mountains and hills, and hearing nothing but the sounds of nature when we stopped the car and turned the engine off, we saw a world that the more adventurous Etruscans, and before them the Umbrian tribes, must have relished before the invading imperialistic Roman legions put them to the sword if they would not submit. I like the way D.H.

Lawrence put it in his book *Etruscan Places*: 'The Etruscans, as everyone knows, were the people who occupied the middle of Italy in early Roman days, and whom the Romans in their usual neighbourly fashion wiped out in order to make room for Rome with a very big R. They couldn't have wiped them all out, there were too many of them. But they did wipe out the Etruscan existence as a nation and as a people.

'However, this seems to be the inevitable result of expansion with a big E, which is the whole *raison d'être* of people like the Romans.'

It was expansion with a big 'E' that forced men like Pliny into spending most of their lives in service to the state, journeying to some of the farthest parts of the empire, forcing him to work at the court in Rome when, if his letters are to be believed, he would rather be in his villa in Tifernum, looking out on that natural amphitheatre created by the foothills of the Apennines. It was this idea of time stolen from a busy and pressured professional life that appealed to me and to other Italians through the centuries. The Merchant of Prato, as Iris Origo tells us, in her magnificent profile of him, got hooked on building a villa away from the pressures of international trade, so much so that he even joined in the physical labour with the bricklayers and the plasterers, much to his friend Ser Lap Mazzei's concern. Lorenzo the Magnificent, almost a century later in the 1490s, built villas galore but chose to die in his favourite at Careggi just outside Florence. A place where, all too infrequently for his taste, he managed to snatch time from the weight of responsibility of being First Citizen of Florence.

As so often happens in Italy, I find that if you talk to enough people, soon the information you seek will be provided. It was much later at an impromptu supper in an old hunting lodge, once belonging to Lorenzo de Medici, that I heard about the ruins being excavated. Beth Romer, another guest, whose book *The Tuscan Year* makes all of us writers about things Italian jealous, was a Pliny fan too . . .

'Have you been to Selci Lama?' she asked. I said I had. I told her about my meeting with the mysterious and perfumed woman in the lonely inn . . .

'You were miles off the route. Do you remember the big *palazzo*, well you turn left at the *palazzo*, and you'll see the outline of the foundations of what they think is Pliny's villa.'

So back I drove one perfect summer's morning in late August, up the *autostrada* from Perugia past Città di Castello, and took the next exit at Selci Lama, as I had done once before. But this time I followed Beth's directions and, sure enough, skirting the wall round the villa I came across the outline of some buildings. A deserted site but obviously one where a fair amount of work had been done. There was a high wire fence around it and a notice telling people like me to keep out . . . this was private property.

It was disappointing. Somehow I didn't feel what H.V. Morton had felt at Pliny's place near Lake Como. I remember reading in James Boswell's diaries of his Italian trip that he was so overcome when he saw the Roman Forum for the first time, he started speaking Latin and couldn't stop. The view looked about right, though. But deep down I wasn't really convinced that this was indeed Pliny's villa, or at least that part of the villa he so lovingly described in his letters . . . with its box hedges, shady walks and the sound of water. As I was standing there, a man came past on a moped and asked if I was lost.

'Is this Pliny's villa?' I asked him.

He looked at me with the tolerance the Italians have developed for foreigners in their land who ask odd questions in the middle of an otherwise normal day.

'Ask at the big house, they'll know,' he said and, wobbling

slightly at the start, he chugged off leaving me in a small cloud of dust kicked up by the new tyres with thick treads that looked as if they had been put on only that morning.

There was no answer from the big house, in fact the big gate was shut and locked. Three metres tall at least, the same height as the wall that surrounded the property. Through a crack in the metalwork, I could see statuary, classical and looking quite old, a bust and a statue, though whether they were real or just modern copies I have not the expert eye to say. Getting no answer, I walked across the narrow road to a group of houses opposite – a jumble of largely untouched buildings that could date from fifty to a hundred and fifty years. A door was open and a huge woman in black was sweeping the narrow hallway inside.

'Is there anyone at home in the big house?' I asked in my best Italian.

'*La marchesa non c'e. E fuori.*'

I wasn't sure I'd heard aright, 'The *marchesa?*' I asked. 'Yes, *la marchesa* Capelleti. She's away.'

I asked if she knew anyone who would let me in. But there was no one. It was best I rang the *marchesa*, the number was in the book.

I stopped off in a café in Selci Lama, and looked up her number in the telephone book . . . sure enough, there she was, *la Marchesa* Capelleti. It's an odd name. It means 'little hats' and in fact is a type of pasta, small pasta shells shaped like hats.

That evening, with Ornella and Sergio Contini, I met Ornella's brother-in-law Giorgio, a huge bear of a man, stooped now because of a compacted vertebra, which makes him look rather the shape of the French actor who was so popular in the fifties, Fernandel of the expressive face. A man who has travelled the world in his time, he too is restoring a house just outside Rome and is as interested in history, especially of the Roman period, because his house is near the Roman centre Ferroniae. Giorgio immediately offered to do some ferreting out of information for me: whether the villa did exist and whether the foundations I had seen near the *marchesa*'s *palazzo* were really Pliny's or some other structure.

Giorgio called me a couple of days later, fuming at what he saw as the indifference and at times rudeness of the Ministry of Culture: he had become bogged down in the bureaucracy of the state system which looks after Italian art and cultural treasures. But he had some numbers for me to call in Perugia. 'More bureaucrats,' he said apologetically.

I decided to take the direct route. I called the *marchesa*'s number myself. A woman's voice answered, the voice of an elderly woman from the sound of it. The voice, sharp and to the point, confirmed that it belonged to the *marchesa* herself. And breaking into English, she asked in a peremptory fashion: 'What do you want?'

I explained my quest for Pliny's villa, and wondered whether she had part of the villa in her grounds, or knew of its whereabouts, or could give me any other information which might be ... She broke into my long and respectful speech with the sharp, 'There's no Pliny villa, no Pliny villa. I cannot help you.' I persisted, could I come and see the house ... But she would have none of it and, in a surprising turn of phrase for an Italian aristocrat, said harshly, 'No bloody Pliny villa here ... do you understand.' The conversation was at an end.

I drove back to Selci Lama the next day, thinking that maybe I would knock on the door and pretend I was someone else, and she might let me in. But I stopped off in Città di Castello this time just to see the place that might have been the main urban centre of our life in Italy, had we opted for the first possible house to restore. Città has a charm which may not be apparent early in the year, when the days are darker and the wind tends to make you turn up your collar in the street and put your head down. In summer, though, the light reveals an interesting old town, where Vasari worked. And Raphael too, as a young painter, left the Perugian workshop of his then master Perugino to paint in the church of San Francesco there. The picture is called the *Marriage of the Virgin* and the original is in Milan at the Brera. But a copy remains and, as I looked at it that day, an old man, who may have been a priest, came and stood next to me.

'It's not real, you know. It's only a copy.' He paused and looked at it again, 'but I still think Raphael would have been pleased with this picture.' I'm sure he would, just as he would have been pleased that they named the square outside after him. The picture itself is famous and looks remarkably like one of the best known pictures of his master Perugino, my hero, which Raphael left untouched when he was asked to paint over some of the original frescos in the Sistine Chapel. That picture was *Christ delivering the keys to St Peter*, painted in 1482. What's interesting is that one of the figures, the only figure in fact to look straight out of the painting at the spectators, for the rest have their eyes on the ceremony of the keys, looks remarkably like Perugino's . . . indeed, some think the face is another self-portrait. There's that red hat, the unkempt hair, the jowly face and the direct stare.

There's another picture by Perugino which is similar in structure, with the same title as the Raphael, which Perugino painted sometime between 1500 and 1504. I say 'painted' but there has been some doubt because, at one time or another, this picture, which is in the Musée des Beaux Arts in Caen, has been attributed to Pintoricchio and even to Raphael himself. But it is the poses that, to my mind, are the key. Perugino has often been criticized by modern art historians for his repetitive style, using the same basic cartoon over and over again, so that his figures always seem to be stuck in one of half a dozen poses – eyes up to the right, eyes up to the left, down to the right, down to the left and so on. Even the hands follow predetermined drawings in which the artist or his assistant made no concession to the subject matter of the work being undertaken. These Peruginoesque poses are there in Raphael's picture but already his skill lifts them beyond anything his master could have achieved.

Yet another interesting question to be answered is to do with the nature of the relationship between master and pupil: in Città della Pieve, in the *Visitation of the Magi*, one of the onlookers in the picture by Perugino is said to be the young Raphael. Were they like father and son, were they lovers . . . such relationships were not unknown.

In Città's art gallery there are more connections with Perugino: the façade was designed by Vasari, who wrote so scathingly of the Umbrian master. There's also work by Luca Signorelli of Cortona, one of Perugino's best friends in the art world, an almost exact contemporary and a drinking buddy.

Before I left Città di Castello, although I saw one more reference to Pliny the Younger as a street name, I realized that I had gone about as far as I wanted to with him. Once again I discovered that my abiding interest outside the house and the land was in the gaps in the life of that enigmatic Umbrian master, Pietro Perugino, born in the little town that was now the commune to which I belonged, Città della Pieve. And who knows, one of these days if I keep reading enough and asking enough people I may be able to prove he really was born in the Valley of the Fireflies. What a day that would be. Yes, *la marchesa* could keep her privacy whether she had the site of Pliny's villa on her land or not.

Pliny had been an interesting and amusing distraction. The

sight of that Raphael, of Vasari and the Signorelli, however, changed my mind and told me to discipline myself a little more if I was to produce a film or book on the greatest of the Umbrian artists and, for me, one of the giants of the Renaissance. And I've kept my word so far. Giorgio had asked I don't know how many people about Pliny's villa on my behalf and finally, when I was back in England after the summer of 1993, I got a call from him with the number of a key person in the cultural affairs office of the regional government of Perugia. This lady would be more than happy to take me to the site and answer any questions I might have. All I had to do was call.

The number and name are still tucked in the back cover of my Loeb edition of Pliny the Younger's letters. One of these days I might make the call and drive up to Città di Castello. Pliny's waited nearly two thousand years for me to discover him. He won't mind waiting a little longer I'm sure. As he himself says so often, there are days when he's in the country that he just likes to follow his own inclination and put off what needs to be done. Who am I to disobey? *Ave atque vale.*

10 The New Republic

ALMOST FIVE YEARS to the day after signing the deed of sale with the Gambacorta sisters I was back in Italy on a BBC assignment, covering the March 1994 elections which ushered in what Italians like to call 'the Second Republic'. In truth, though, I sometimes find it hard to see the difference between them: the First Republic managed to survive more than fifty governments in the forty-eight years or so of its existence and the political horse trading surrounding the creation of the first government of the new era was extremely intense.

As I write, the Second Republic is more a hope than a political fact for, as the Italians say, 'you can change the conductor, but the music stays the same'. Less polite, but far more expressive is the even more pithy Roman remark, passed on to me by the BBC's Southern Europe correspondent, Matt Frei, who is based in the Italian capital: 'The politicians may have changed their suits, but they have kept the same underwear.'

This trip was the first time that I had exposed myself to Italian politics at their most raw and vibrant. Until then, I had largely avoided the subject, having my fill of it back home with the endless succession of politicians through the *Today* studio who tended to be, how can I put it tactfully, not a little repetitious in their pushing of policy. Italy had been the antidote to all that. For the first five years, as we established ourselves on a part-time basis in Italy, we were obsessed with getting the house and the land into some sort of order. Obsessed to the point of shutting out almost everything else.

Inevitably, the political dimension was something which we ignored. Around friends' tables for supper or lunch, the main, indeed the only political references were to politicians as thieves and, in the First Republic, not only thieves but exceptionally greedy thieves. In many ways most Italians of our acquaintance seemed to accept that the system left room for a little lining of pockets but that one was expected to be discreet and not have your pockets so full that everyone could see what you had been doing. Soon the pockets were overflowing – it was time for suitcases. As charge after charge was brought, as more and more investigations were launched, so Italians became obsessed with what was called 'clean hands'. A Milanese judge, Antonio di Pietro, became a hero and a TV star as he prosecuted those who had dipped their hands too deeply into government finance. Di Pietro, in his courtroom gown with the gold tassels would, night after night on prime time television, display the whole range of emotions from incredulity, to anger, to pleasure, to understanding, to toughness. There wasn't a gesture or a facial expression missing in his repertoire. It was always a grand-standing performance. He was the George Carman of the Italian justice system, with the thespian skills of a Laurence Olivier. We hardly watched television so the TV coverage of the bribe trial was a sideshow for us. But when we caught the programmes, we were hooked. We had never given a bribe and, if one had been given on our behalf by Giancarlo, he had the good manners not to tell us about it.

We obeyed Voltaire's dictum in *Candide* that we would have a happy life if we just 'cultivated our Garden' and let the rest pass us by. Of course there could not be a complete intellectual vacuum. Italy does not allow that, which is why I spent most of my spare time trying to track down new facts about the life of Perugino. For me Italian politics meant the politics of the fifteenth century, from the pragmatic theories of Machiavelli, to the guile of men like Lorenzo di Medici and the rampant nepotism of the Borgias. All set in the context of a dazzling time when the arts were put at the service of the rich and powerful and used as much for comfort as for the effect they had on their rivals for power. Indeed so deep was I in the books that I was but barely aware that Italy was moving from one republic to another in the last decade of the twentieth century. There were parallels, though, that I soon began to see. The corruption of the Church was a kind of fifteenth century Tangentopoli, the name given to Milan, 'Bribe City'. Then, as now, corruption brought about massive retribution to the political class that had put its snout in the trough. In those more violent less squeamish times it came in the form of the sack of Rome by the Germans in a week long orgy of murder, rape and pillage in 1527. Today it took the form of ridicule by one's peers and cross-examination by prosecutors in the court rooms in Milan and Rome. For someone for whom politics was part of the daily journalistic round, Italy was a worrying reminder that there is more to life than wondering whether Kenneth Clarke would succeed John Major or whether Michael Heseltine could make a surprising late run and win the poisoned chalice. Mr Heseltine, who once told me politely on the programme to get off his back when I asked him whether he was still interested in the leadership, would probably hope that all the BBC's interviewers would get places in Umbria if the feeling I was beginning to develop was the result.

Up until the elections in March 1994 our time in Italy had consisted of reading almost anything I could lay my hands on in the evenings, while by day doing the real work on land and house. That March was warmer than usual, so the plants were beginning to shoot ahead in the warm sun and the pergola, which over the winter we had doubled in size, was soon looking quite striking as the vine and the wisteria shoots began their annual battle for supremacy on the wooden beams. The fields too seemed much more colourful, perhaps we had more time now to appreciate the yellows, the purples, and white and blues of the daisy, dandelions and other flowers which cover every inch of soil.

Given our country idyll, perhaps I should have refused the *Today* assignment. Now I can say I'm glad I did accept it, though I also have to say that ten days on the road talking to politicians and pundits about whether Italy would change if the Right or the Left won made me feel for the first time that the expectation of maintaining a retreat in such a climate and country had been unrealistic.

Part of the worry came from the intensely political time and my background reading about the way in which the Left and the Right were set to fight to the bitter end for power. The way most writers wrote their scenarios, it was either communism or fascism that was on offer – extremes that Italy hadn't faced for half a century. And that worry was reinforced by a book I read on the plane out. I bought it because of the simple title *The Villa*. People in my trade can always read more into our research than is perhaps wise . . . lines and thoughts take on a significance which seem certain at the time but, in retrospect, are not as meaningful as they seemed when faced with the need to fill time on air, or column inches in print.

Perhaps it was what the author had to say about people like me owning houses like mine, in a glossy text wrapped around lovely pictures of Palladian and other types of Italian villas that got to me. The author in question is the architectural historian James A. Ackerman. He writes at length in his book about what he calls the ideology of villas, not in the modern political sense but in the sense of a concept or myth. And he goes on to point out: 'Today as in the past the farmer and the peasant, whether poor and oppressed or rich and independent, do not as a rule regard country life as an idyllic state, but accept it as a necessary and often somewhat antipathetic condition. In the folklore of all ages, the country dweller, with some misgivings, has longed for the stimulation and the comforts of city life. The city dweller on the other hand, has typically idealised country life, and when means are available, has sought to acquire property in which it might be enjoyed. This impulse is generated by psychological rather than utilitarian needs . . .' and he concludes, 'the villa . . . is a myth or fantasy through which over the course of millennia persons whose position of privilege is rooted in urban commerce and industry have been able to expropriate rural land, often requiring, for the realisation of the myth, the care of a labouring class or of slaves.' Note that worrying word 'expropriate', and remember the way the Gambacorta sisters thought they had been ripped off when they saw how we had developed their property and increased its value. All of which, on the eve of an historic election suddenly put the Hobdays' Umbrian property into a very different perspective.

As I say, the trouble was that I had happened on this book just before I left for Italy, when all the best informed opinion told me Italy was breaking apart and that the Left and the Right would take no prisoners. Inevitably, in that atmosphere, the political nature of Ackerman's last sentence was not lost on me, especially since it was obvious that the centre was about to disappear in the forthcoming elections. The old consensus, which had kept out the communists on the Left and the neo-fascists on the Right, had been destroyed by the scandals, with former prime ministers like Giulio Andreotti, of the Christian Democrats, being accused of being in the pay of, if not actually a member of, the mafia, and other former prime ministers, like Bettino Craxi, the socialist, of having syphoned off party finances to friends and colleagues, one of whom, Gianni di Michelis, I was to meet.

If the Right won, would they tolerate so many foreigners in the country? Had there been foreign property owners hanged by Mussolini's blackshirts, I wondered. If the Left won, would they tolerate so many foreigners taking away people's homes? Had the Soviets put foreign capitalists in labour camps?

As it was a subject near to my heart, I suggested to the producer Richard Clark that the trip should take in the questions of racism and crime, both of which would be key areas of difference between the two political extremes. As a precaution, I looked up Yeats's poem, 'The Second Coming', about the centre not holding, the best lacking all conviction and mere anarchy being loosed upon the world, so that we would have a suitably literary quote if the need arose. Luckily, for the sake of *Today* listeners – and yours truly – we did not need to use it.

The editor Roger Mosey was persuaded and the *Today* programme financed a trip that took in a refugee camp for Bosnians just inside the Italian border with Slovenia, not far from Trieste in the north east; politicians from both extremes in Venice; down to mafia-spotting in Palermo in Sicily, before ending up in Rome to broadcast live from the makeshift studio in the BBC's offices in the Piazza del Collegio Romano. I met members of all the main parties contesting the election, from the federalists of the northern league to the progressives, who were mainly former communists who had changed their party name but whose enemies on the Right claimed had not changed their collectivist policies one jot. And of course I met members of the political phenomenon of these elections, candidates and party workers of Forza Italia, Silvio Berlusconi's creation, which won such an astounding victory after less than one hundred days of active political existence and campaigning.

As I say, usually on such assignments, the political outcome is interesting in a rather academic way but of no direct or personal concern. What you want are dramatic headlines: 'Italy on the Brink,' or a stylish piece of alliteration, 'Violence on the Via Venato'. Happily, there was no violence on the Via Venato. However, as I sat in the basement conference room of the curiously named Jolly Hotel just off that very street at around one o'clock on election night, jostled by cameramen, photographers and other foreign correspondents, waiting for Il Cavaliere (the Knight), as Berlusconi had been nicknamed, to arrive to make his victory speech, I could not help but wonder whether my house a hundred miles north of Rome, in a quiet Umbrian valley, would be untouched.

And when, walking along the Corso much later that fresh spring night watching the wealthy youngsters drive their fast sports cars, sounding their horns, and some of them, I hope only for the benefit of the TV cameras, giving a triumphant fascist salute, I felt genuinely alarmed.

It was at these moments and for a few days following that reality intruded on the myth of the sun-kissed rural residence in a Mediterranean country where, as Pliny says, 'You don't have to wear a toga and it is always quiet and peaceful'. The problem for the centre of Italy, and for Umbria in particular, is that it is still overwhelmingly a left-wing region politically. While the rest of Italy moved to the Right, my fellow Umbrians stayed firmly with the Left. *Corriere dell'Umbria* summarized their views in an article just a couple of days after the vote: while the national government promised less state control and more market forces, what would that do for a small marginal region like Umbria? Here there was a recession and the majority reckoned the only way the place would survive was through central government providing the financial means.

To put it in very simple terms, would the olives that I harvest after Berlusconi's win be pressed in a co-operative venture with all my neighbours, like last year? Or would private enterprise move in and, by competing with the co-operative, at first make it cheaper for me but then, having driven out the old subsidized oil press, exploit their monopoly by pushing up the prices? Well, that's what some of my neighbours said would happen. When I talked to some of the locals they saw it in very Italian terms, why should a right-wing government bother with a left-wing region, a region where the Left had polled nearly 50 per cent, while the Right had just over 35 per cent? I wondered as I read the *Corriere dell'Umbria* that day whether it was a good idea to send three trade union leaders to see Silvio Berlusconi to talk about the future. Berlusconi's Forza Italia was, in British terms, of the Thatcherite school of economics . . . so there was unlikely to be any red wine and *panini* (the Italian equivalent of beer and sandwiches) waiting for them when they got to his offices.

While the Left still dominates my part of Umbria, indeed the whole region, there was one other worrying electoral statistic in the paper, and this was the Alleanza Nazionale, the national alliance party, and one which its enemies claimed is neo-fascist and which had polled the third highest in the region. I attended their eve of election rally in the Piazza del Popolo in Rome to hear Gianfranco Fini speak. This donnish bespectacled man in the dark suit cuts a figure that is at odds with what his enemies claim he represents. Fini might rhyme with Mussolini but there is no swaggering *braggadocio* in this man, no strutting, no posing. The crowd had come to cheer whatever he said, however he stood on the platform above them. Much to Fini's discomfort, there was no mistaking the fascists salutes from the younger element in the massive crowd that completely filled the square. As the leader stepped forward, to the music of 'The Chorus of the Hebrew Slaves' from the opera *Nabucco*, the arms rose and fell in salute. The young toughs, many with shaved heads, chanted Fi-ni, Fi-ni . . . the arm goes up on the syllable 'Fi', . . . drops after a second on the syllable 'ni' and is repeated until a crescendo of noise merges into applause and cheering. Fini raises his arms from the podium, floodlit, with the Italian flags all in a row behind him. Via the microphone and the massive loudspeaker system come his first words, '*Romani* . . .' more cheers, '*Romani* . . . tonight your presence here is concrete evidence of what the people want. They want change, they are against crime, and dirt . . .' and so it went on.

Standing alongside me in the crowd in the Piazza del Popolo that evening was a young couple in their early twenties, smartly dressed, both with jobs from the look of them. Married or engaged, I'm not certain, but together for sure. So far they've restricted themselves to cheering. But when Fini finishes on a particular flourish of nationalism, their eyes are bright and wide with excitement. They hesitate for a second and then almost lose control before joining with others in the salute. They were having a mutual political orgasm.

The next day I visited one of Fini's candidates, Gustavo Selva, in his constituency office in the narrow Via della Lupa in Rome. The silverhaired old gentleman took my hand and said, 'My dear friend, don't be misled by all this talk of neo-fascism. We are democrats. We hate dictatorship. We have fought it in the past, it will never come back.'

I believed him because I wanted to believe him, this former journalist, the man who used to run one of the state television networks. His office was in the Via della Lupa, as I say. I looked up the word just to make sure I understood. It means the street of the wolf. But still I asked myself, should we worry?

There's a story, I don't know how true, that even in my small village in Umbria, many years ago, the fascists had planted a bomb which exploded in the local bar. Moiano is virtually one hundred per cent communist, or rather 'progressive' as it calls itself today when it votes. Yet the memories of that outrage are still fresh for the older generation, as are the memories of what Italians call the 'years of lead' in the late seventies and early eighties, when the Red Brigades were at their most violent. Let me give you some chilling statistics which a neighbour of ours in Umbria collected for her book on Italian terrorism. Alison Jamieson lives about a forty-minute drive away from us, near Pozzuolo, in a house not unlike ours, with her husband Nigel, an acknowledged expert on one of the more acceptable faces of Italy, opera. Alison says that between 1969 and 1987, 14,591 terrorist attacks were committed in Italy, injuring nearly 1,200 people, killing 419. What is even more chilling is that 193 deaths are attributed to the Right and 145 to the Left, almost even; the other deaths are attributed to Middle East terrorist groups. Alison's book, *The Heart Attacked* was published in the year we bought the house.

I suppose we should take comfort that an internationally recognized authority on political terrorism should have chosen to live where we are in Italy. Alison, I like to believe, came here because she thought it was safe. But then are doctors their own best physicians? Since we bought, the main violence has been from the mafia which, under the leadership of the *capo dei capi*, Toto Riina has been fighting what even Italians call a war with the state. There have been what Gerry Adams of Sinn Fein would no doubt call 'spectaculars', such as those outrages in which judges Falcone and Borsellino were blown up in Sicily, Falcone with his wife on his way in from the airport to Palermo and Borsellino had just left his mother's flat in the centre of that city.

What I had to hope for on my assignment was that the reassuring words uttered by some of my interviewees would hold good ... that while on the surface it might look like change and possibly dangerous change, beneath the surface, Italy was the same as she had always been. But I had to guard against the false hopes of the citizen who doesn't want to get involved and preserve the objective view of the professional reporter looking on life as it is, rather than as others think or hope it is. At times it was difficult to separate the two parts of the person that was me, local resident and foreign correspondent. It's a measure, I suppose, of how quickly I have put down roots in my other home. I would have felt the same, I guess, if the political battle in Britain became as divisive and bitter as the last days of this election were to become.

Let's start though with the more optimistic views on Italy in the nineties. The most encouraging analysis came during an hour passed with one of Italy's yesterday's men. Gianni di Michelis had been foreign minister, but is still rather better known for his nightclubbing and dancing in all the best spots in Venice, his home town, and in Rome. During his days in power, it is said, he lived at the Plaza Hotel in Rome all expenses paid . . . or rather not paid. The hotel is still waiting for the Socialist Party to pay the bill, say some observers of the political scene. It's such a good story I have not checked it out.

We met in his small apartment in the Piazza di Pietra in the heart of Rome's Centro Storico. Gone were the flunkeys of old, the helpers and the hangers on. Di Michelis lives alone now in his top-floor flat and opened the door himself to let us in. He looked a little less sleek than when at the height of his political career but the long, black curly hair was still there, dropping over the open collar of a slightly crumpled white shirt.

He murmured some apologies for the state of the apartment. 'I'm alone now . . .' he said and shrugged his shoulders. Pictures crowded one wall, books filled the others and, in an alcove just off the main room, was a table piled high with newspapers, books and a small PC balanced precariously on top. I remember he had two huge television sets, side by side, and a mass of videos – some of news programmes in which he featured no doubt – crammed underneath them. I don't think it's premature to call him 'yesterday's man', though anything is possible in Italian politics. Yet here he was, one of the architects of the European Union and would be peacemakers in Bosnia, very much on his own.

In many ways, however, he was the right man to talk to about Italy and Italian politics: he had been an insider and, as such, could better tell me in the most disinterested way about the political realities of the country in which for the moment I lived part time but hoped one day to make my home. Better still from the broadcaster's point of view, his English is not only fluent but his huge vocabulary allows him nuances which I would have missed had he tried to speak to me in his own tongue, and would have diminished what he had to say had his English been less capable.

His main thesis was that Italy was purely and simply going through a power struggle. He said, however, that it was maybe neither really pure nor simple in the sense that, given the stakes, every trick in the political manual of war was being used. The Italians, it must be said, give very full answers ... they warm to the subject and the more you nod in understanding or appreciation, the more they will add yet another flourish, another metaphor, another word to intrigue you and demolish any counter-arguments you may have thought you had.

Let me précis: what Italy has lost, says di Michelis, is the old equilibrium; the old political framework has been destroyed, by the parties themselves, helped by the judges and public opinion. But what one has to remember is that this is not about the new replacing the old, for they are all of the ancien régime, apart from Umberto Bossi, the leader of the Lega, the federalist party in the north. Not even Berlusconi is a new man, says di Michelis: 'He may be new to politics,' but as a leading businessman, 'he is not new to the system.' This was reinforced a few months later when Berlusconi's business empire and his brother Paolo became embroiled in the bribes scandal.

I asked whether he accepted that he and men like him were to blame for the corruption that brought about the end of the 'political equilibrium' of 1948 to 1993. It's too early, he claimed, for history to judge who was to blame or who was innocent. 'As in any power struggle there are victims.' Nor did he accept that the old system had been a total failure ... the Italian economy had its problems as every European national economy, but a great deal of progress had been made. Nor indeed was there a crisis of democracy, the vote is going ahead, the system is changing within a parliamentary system.

Di Michelis made a persuasive defence of the ancien régime but then, as Mandy Rice–Davies would have said, 'He would have said that wouldn't he.' He muddied the waters sufficiently, however, for me to wonder how many of the judges were of left-wing political motivation in their rush to investigate members of certain political parties. As the former foreign minister would have it, the communists breached a tacit agreement about party financing and launched a power struggle to topple the centre-left alliance and win power for themselves. At moments like this the foreigners' eyes tend to glaze over at the intricacy of Italian politics, and even in English the language becomes strained. Much of the debate is formalized around words like reform, development, freedom and justice, with my favourite Italian political catchphrase of the late Aldo Moro (murdered you may recall by the Red Brigades), 'converging parallels', thrown in for good measure. They all say much the same. In the end the key to politics in Italy is more the personality of the leaders, the charismatic individuals around whom the groupings form, not the detail of the policies which seem intentionally vague, because it's the civil servants who run the country day by day. It has always been thus, from Roman times when family clans fought for supremacy to the Renaissance city states, where dukes, princes, cardinals and their families fought for advantage. It's the people, not the policies that count in this part of the world, and who can work with whom, or who will work against whom, with one of the leaders eventually emerging as prime minister.

Di Michelis was once such a man, but now he has been pushed aside. So what of the new men? Among others, I talked to one of the most charming but oddest politicians on the Right. To some he is as nutty as a fruitcake, to others he is the future. Franco Rochetta is federal president of the Northern League and founder of the Venetian League, one of the small federal parties that make up the Northern League.

Rochetta is of medium height, balding, slight of build and quietly spoken. He seems to frown with worry at some impending disaster, rarely smiling, always trying to do two things at once. Like so many modern Italians, he carries that essential accessory for the successful man, a cellular phone. Our conversation was interrupted on a regular basis by its persistent ringing. As a student, in the heady days of 1968, he had espoused the cause of an independent Veneto region: for him the days when each region of Italy governed itself were the days when Italy was happiest and most successful. That history might suggest otherwise – the wars between Milan, Florence, Pisa, Perugia and Papal Rome, not to mention the shifting alliances necessary to keep Venice afloat – did not dissuade Rochetta of the essential truth of his position.

'Was not Venice a world power when she governed herself? Did not Florence become the envy of the world? And Sicily, did not Sicily exist as a great kingdom?'

For Rochetta the modern Italian state, unified by Garibaldi, and supported in a referendum by over 90 per cent of the population – every town and city square has the numbers of the majority for unity carved in stone – the modern Italian state was taking money from the rich regions and using it to line centralist politicians' pockets and for the crime syndicates of the *mezzogiorno* and Sicily.

As we drove from Venice to a political meeting at the centuries-old University of Padua (one of the first in Europe), Rochetta spoke of his fear of the Left and the communist conspiracy to run the country as a centrally directed state. One telling moment, when we stopped at lights on the outskirts of the beautiful city of Padua, was the arrival of the inevitable young African offering to clean the windscreen. Rochetta waved him away and said without prompting that he was part of an invasion, planned by the Left to swamp the country. This must be stopped, he said, for 'when the Germans threatened to invade Britain, you British fought back . . . we must do the same.' I suggested that there could be racism in what he was saying.

'I am not racist. My father was in a German concentration camp for two years. I could not be racist. What I want is for people to live with dignity in their own countries, not be exploited by being shipped into countries like ours for political ends.'

I recalled that conversation the next day after a long drive out of Venice towards Trieste and the border with Slovenia. This whole area has been fought over many times, captured by Mussolini, some given back after the war, and Trieste occupied for a time by what was then Yugoslavia. I was to visit a refugee camp, the Campo Purgessima, just a handful of kilometres from the border. This old army barracks was now home to two hundred Bosnian Muslims, men, women and children. Some had been there for over two years, hoping either for a visa to go to America, the dream of most, or to Italy. None wanted to go back to Bosnia, where the man I spoke to said he had been in a concentration camp. Sloven Saric came from Capcjana in Bosnia. He was, I guess, in his late twenties, but his eyes looked much older. He was the only refugee, as far as I could discover, who spoke any English. He was skeletal, his dark hair close-cropped, his teeth rotten through bad diet, and smoking a permanent cigarette. All of them, said Mr Saric, feared a victory by the Lega under Bossi in particular and the Right in general.

'Once you've been in a concentration camp, you know that anything can happen to you. Anything, even the very worst of things. The Right don't want us here.'

Back in Venice, Adreana Vigneri, a gentle-looking intellectual and candidate for the progressives, was also worried at the
prospect of a right-wing victory. Not so much because of any
racist tendencies on the part of the Right, though she feared
them of course, but because the taxation policies suggested by
Berlusconi and the rest meant that the poor south would
suffer, as the rich north paid but a small proportion of the
revenue it raised to the central government. Indeed, this was
the crux of the Left-Right battle. The Right wanted local
taxes used locally, the Left wanted the old system to continue.
If the Right wins, said Vigneri, then Italy will break apart.

Much of this was election rhetoric but Umberto Bossi fought
hard in the days after Berlusconi's team had won to get a new
constitution in which some form of federalism would be
enshrined. For Franco Rochetta such a move would crown a
lifetime of political struggle on the fringes. For Vigneri, it
would be her worst nightmare come true. For me, in little
Umbria, a region the size of Wales with 800,000 inhabitants, it
could mean local services deteriorating, hospitals closing and
the emigration of the young in search of work to the big cities
of the north. No wonder the first words Maria Pazzaglia said
to me, when I got back after the trip around Italy, were that
the result had 'frightened' her.

It has to be said that my pre-election journey around Italy
also took in Sicily. It was a place I'd always wanted to visit.
My late brother John spent the last few years of his life in
Agrigento, near the famous Valley of the Temples, and he's
buried there. This time I didn't get to Agrigento but went
first to Palermo, and then did a two-hour drive to a place with
a name which is now world famous because of a series of mafia
films from America, Corleone. We went there because it is the
home town of Toto Riina, now in prison, but for ten years the
Capo de capi, the don of all the dons. In a bookshop near the

cathedral, where well he might once have worshipped, I bought the story of his criminal career from an old man who murmured, 'He's not as bad as he's painted you know.'

The purpose of the trip, throughout Italy as well as in Sicily, was to see whether Italy was changing. There was a symbolic answer to be found in the town square of this small bustling market town set in the central hills of this enchanting island. The old square, like so many squares the length and breadth of the republic, had been named after Garibaldi. Now it had been renamed Falcone and Borsellino Square. The mayor, who had thought the change of name would help change the reputation of his town, was to receive a special message from the mafia for his pains – a severed bull's head left one night on his front doorstep.

Back in Palermo in the gilded town hall, with its gold, silk-flock wallpapers, portraits and busts of mayors of yesteryear, I met a man who had come to prominence and the mayor's job because of his anti-mafia stance. Leoluca Orlando, who is a lawyer but looks more like a professor, talked with confidence on the eve of an election which was to remove his party, the Rete (the Network), from national politics. He too feared the Right coming to power with the help of the mafia. That day the *Giornale di Sicilia* had published the findings of a Rome-based institute for political, social and economic research, Eurispes, which reckoned that one in ten candidates of all parties were supported by the mafia. Eurispes also claimed that there were some half a million Italians linked with the mafia: 100,000 full-time professionals and about 400,000 part-timers or bit players. The election campaign itself saw accusations of mafia involvement in all parties, even a Berlusconi aide was being investigated. As Mayor Orlando pointed out, the mafia has no politics as such, they want protection from whoever is in power, so if the polls were showing that Forza

Italia was likely to be a winner, then the mafia would want to be involved somehow. The mafia story seems a long way from Umbria, thankfully, but if the report is right about the numbers of Italians linked with such an organization there is presumably nowhere to hide.

That the mafia can co-exist with the legitimate power structure in the country is beyond question. In Palermo itself, where the anti-mafia forces are at their strongest, Riina himself lived for twenty years in a house on a piece of land in the centre of Palermo. The land had been bought by the city to develop as a conference centre. In his final years of freedom, Riina is said to have lived there almost full time in a typical *contadino*'s house, tending his olives, growing his vine and ordering the killing of Falcone and Borsellino and no doubt even Andreotti's best friend and representative on the island, Salvatore Lima.

The last time the Right was in power, under Mussolini's fascists, the mafia had almost been wiped out, until the Americans at the end of the Second World War had used them to help chase the Germans from the island, thus saving the organization from total extinction. This time one wonders whether the Right will be as tough or can be as tough. Mussolini's was a one-party state. Berlusconi had to try to keep his three-party alliance together, until election night, let alone beyond that and into government.

There's one man I would have liked to have met on this trip across Italy, had he still been living. Luigi Barzini, in that classic analysis of his nation, *The Italians*, writes at the end of his book: 'The unsolved problems pile up and produce catastrophes at regular intervals. The Italians always see the next one coming with a clear eye, but like sleepers in a nightmare, cannot do anything to ward it off. They can play their amusing games, try to secure their families against the coming storm and delude themselves with the thought that, when the smoke clears, Italy can rise again like a phoenix from the ashes. Has she not always done so?'

Those words were written in 1964, thirty years before the coming of the so-called Second Republic. They are as true now as they were then. And they are the words which all my friends in Umbria would no doubt echo fervently.

By an odd juxtaposition of time and date, these crucial elections took place one week before Easter, in many ways the biggest of the holidays in Italy. It's a weekend of seriously socializing, for families and friends, and also of street festivals. A lot of the festivity is centred around the Church, celebrating the proof as it sees it of the Christian faith, the resurrection of Jesus. Inevitably, the metaphor is applied to Italy in its present state, just as Barzini did thirty years ago. On Easter Saturday, the BBC assignment over, we drove over to Petrignano, to the small apartment Sergio Contini shares with Maria. No one mentioned the elections or the result until I asked Sergio what he thought. He shrugged his shoulders.

'No surprise to me,' he says, 'look, we've been brainwashed for nearly fifty years into believing that the Left must never be given power in this country. The Christian Democrats are finished, so there is no centre, so who else can we vote for. As Bossi said to his supporters, "Hold your nose and vote for the Right."'

On Easter Sunday, we went to a much bigger gathering at Sergio's sister's house. Ornella, as always, had outdone herself: nearly twenty people, covering three generations, around the table that evening. And yet such was the joy of the family that if there were any worries about the future, none of it showed.

Giorgio Polumeni, I think as much out of politeness as from any real interest, asked me what I thought of the election result. By way of a reply, I asked him whether he thought it had changed anything.

'I doubt it, but Berlusconi is a bright man, he might do something. But he's not a politician so we may well have another election before the year is out.'

Somebody else said, with a resigned shrug 'They're all politicians, it has nothing to do with us. We let them get on with it.'

Easter Monday dawned bright and sunny, so we decided to go to Città della Pieve for the traditional 'living pictures' show, where some of the local townspeople dress up to portray scenes from the Bible. This being Easter, the scenes were of Our Lord's Passion, the Last Supper, Crucifixion and the Resurrection. Once again I was struck by the faces, which Perugino would have recognized had he still been there to paint them. And the scenes, too, could have come from his brush. Outside, in the main square, the election hoardings, hideous aluminium walls erected especially for the parties to stick their posters, had been taken away. Città was back doing its bit for the record number of tourists in Italy for Easter 1994. I bumped into Valerio Bitarello, the cultural officer, whose job could be at risk with a Thatcherite-style government installed. But he looked confident that he would still be there for the foreseeable future. Umbria had voted the right way, that is Left. And already the right-wing electoral alliance was in the process of breaking up.

By Tuesday, apart from the front pages doing their bit for democracy by publicizing every twist and turn of Silvio Berlusconi's attempts to form a government, the main news was that the miraculous statue of the Blessed Virgin had cried again this Easter and the biggest worry was that over fifty people had died on the roads. At just after nine, a builder came round to talk about a bit of paving we were having laid alongside the house. And Marino arrived with his lorry and nineteen more laurel bushes to be planted. (Victoria had been digging into her secret garden fund again.) None of us mentioned politics.

On the evening before we left for London, I took a last drive round the countryside. I chugged down the hill in a rented Fiat, past the old shed at the bottom which is a veritable museum of Umbria's farming history, with its store of old wagon wheels, the sides of a wagon, an old plough which would have been drawn by white oxen and some of those wooden barrels which the olive and grape pickers use. All of it there, no doubt in case the politicians completely mucked up the country and it was back to the old ways to survive. I took the old country lane up to San Biagio on the other side of the Valley of the Fireflies, to look down on my house. As I climbed up the bumpy dirt track, I almost collided with two old women skinning a rabbit they had trapped for supper. One held it, while the other pulled the skin away. The entrails were hanging out, and a small dog was trying to jump up and grab them. My arrival gave him his chance.

I then took the drive over to Castiglione del Lago, shiny almost in the evening sun on its proud promontory which juts out into Lake Trasimeno. The little town was busy getting ready for the evening's jollities for the Spring Festival, called *Sagra de tulipano*, the blessing of the tulip, which parades round the old centre and the *taverne*, where you can eat a lot for very little. *Gnocchi* in a meat sauce, for example, at under two pounds and a litre of the local wine for under a pound. I bumped into the local picture-framer, who said he'd found a nice old print of the lake I might like to look at.

'It's the view of Tuoro,' he explained, 'roughly where Hannibal slaughtered the 15,000 Roman soldiers.' I told him I'd think about it.

I bought a paper from the newsagent in his little shop underneath the restored belltower in the small square and then walked to the old fort and climbed up to the ramparts to look out over the lake in the evening sun. The water was a mixture of pale translucent blues, with glints of silver where the sun caught a ripple. There was hardly any wind. As I looked out over the old olive groves, I never realized that nature had quite so many shades of green on her palette. I took the car back along the route which skirts the lake, where some fishermen were already hoping to land 'the queen' for supper.

The sun was setting now, deep and orange on my right-hand side, as I drove back home. Past the neatly tilled fields, past the houses with the geraniums beginning to show in the pots at the window. Spring really was here, and the year was starting to pulse to a faster rhythm. How different was the beat of the drum the politicians were marching to down in Rome.

Suddenly I knew that Italy would not change dramatically, my house would still be there when I came back, and my friends. I could go back to start another year of *Today* certain of an Italian future much like the previous five years that I'd spent putting down roots in the place.

If I'm wrong, well, that's another story.

Bibliography

These are just some of the books I read and found useful when writing *In the Valley of the Fireflies*. I've grouped them by subject matter.

Travellers to Italy and the Mediterranean
Michael Adams, *Umbria*, Bellew Books
J.W. Goethe, *Italian Journey*, Penguin Books
H.V. Morton, *A Traveller in Italy*, Methuen
D.H. Lawrence, *Etruscan Places* and *Twilight in Italy*, Penguin Books
Tobias Smollett, *Travels Through Italy and France*, Oxford University Press
Lawrence Durrell, *Bitter Lemons* and *Sense of Place*, Faber & Faber
Cesare de Seta, *L'Italia del Grand Tour*, Electa, Napoli, Italy
James Boswell, *The Grand Tour 1765–76*, Heinemann
Mary McCarthy, *The Stones of Florence*, Penguin Books

Italy Past and Present
Luigi Barzini, *The Italians*, Hamish Hamilton
Peter Nichols, *Italia, Italia*, Macmillan
Alan Friedman, *Agnelli and the Network of Power*, Mandarin
Sergio Romano, *L'Italia Scappata di Mano*, Longanelli, Italy
Alison Jamieson, *The Heart Attacked*, Marion Boyars

Food and Cooking
Apicius, translated by Joseph Dommers Vehling, *Cooking and Dining in Imperial Rome*, Dover
Giacomo Castelvetro (1614), translated by Gillian Riley, *The Fruit, Herbs and Vegetables of Italy*, Viking
Antonio Carluccio, *An Invitation to Italian Cooking*, Pan
Antonella Santolini, *Umbria in Bocca*, La Nuova Edristi, Italy
Jane Dolamore, *The Essential Olive Oil Companion*, Macmillan
Elizabeth Romer, *The Tuscan Year*, Weidenfeld & Nicholson

Gardening
Yves Menzies, *Mediterranean Gardening*, John Murray
Tom Williamson, *Dowsing*, Robert Hale

225

Biography

Christopher Hibbert, *The Rise and Fall of the Medici*, Penguin Books
Iris Origo, *The Merchant of Prato*, Penguin Books
Giorgio Vasari, translated by George Bull, *Lives of the Artists*, Penguin Books
Fiorello Canuti, *Il Perugino*, Editrice d'Arte 'La Diana', Siena, Italy
Pietro Scarpellini, *Perugino*, Electa, Italy
Clare Robertson, *Alessandro Farnese, Il Gran Cardinale*, Yale

Art and Architecture

Cennino d'Andrea Cennini, translated by Daniel V. Thompson, *The Craftsman's Handbook (Il Libro dell'Arte)*, Dover
James A. Ackerman, *The Villa*, Thames and Hudson
Paul Holberton, *Palladio's Villas*, John Murray
Peter Murray, *The Architecture of the Renaissance*, Thames and Hudson
Anthony Osler McIntyre, *Medieval Tuscany and Umbria*, Penguin Books, architectural guides for travellers
Hall's Dictionary of Symbols in Art, John Murray
Jacob Burckhardt, *The Civilisation of the Renaissance*, Penguin Books
John Hale, *The Civilisation of Europe in the Renaissance*, Harper Collins
Frederick Hartt, *History of Italian Renaissance Art*, Thames and Hudson
Bernard Berenson, *Italian Painters of the Renaissance*, Phaidon
John Ruskin, *Writings on Italy and Art*, Penguin Books
Ottavia Niccoli, *Prophecy and People in Renaissance Italy*, Princeton
William Manchester, *A World Lit Only By Fire*, Little, Brown

Classical Sources

IN THE LOEB CLASSICAL LIBRARY, HARVARD UNIVERSITY PRESS
Virgil: *Minor Poems*
Columella
Cato and Varro
Pliny the Elder
Pliny the Younger
Horace
Plutarch

On the great battle of Trasimeno when 15,000 Romans were slaughtered by Hannibal in three hours:

Leonard Cottrell, *Hannibal Enemy of Rome*, Da Capo Press, New York

Livy, *The War with Hannibal*, Penguin Classics.

Finally, a book which gives a marvellous sense of the Roman world and its history:

Ronald Mellor, *Tacitus*, Routledge

General Reading

Alessandro Manzoni, *The Betrothed*, Penguin Books

Stendhal, *The Charterhouse of Parma*, Penguin Books

Italo Calvino, *The Road to San Giovanni*, Cape, and *Italian Folk Tales*, Penguin Books

Rosetta Loy, *The Dust Roads of Monferrato*, Flamingo

Michael Dibdin, *Ratking* and *Cabal*, Faber & Faber

Primo Levi, *The Periodic Table*, Abacus

Index

Index

Index

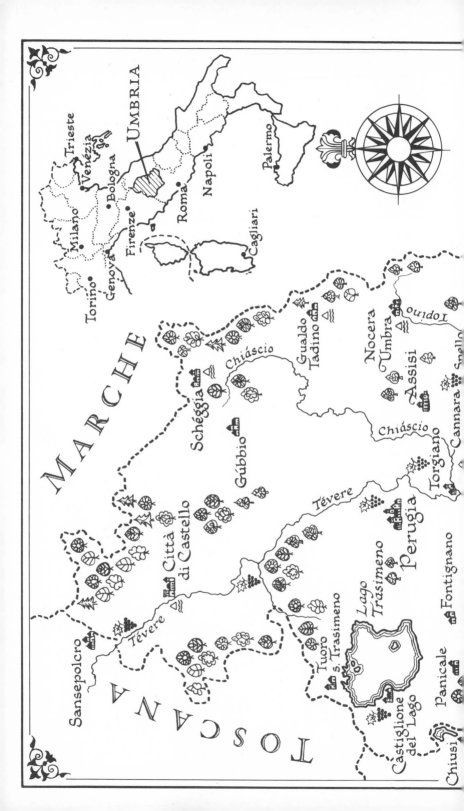